THE GOOD, THE BAD, AND THE DATA

D0781528

for

J   B   E

♥ ♥ *my little units of analysis...*

THE GOOD, THE BAD, AND THE DATA

SHANE THE LONE ETHNOGRAPHER'S ★BASIC★ GUIDE TO QUALITATIVE DATA ANALYSIS

★SALLY CAMPBELL GALMAN★

Routledge
Taylor & Francis Group
LONDON AND NEW YORK

First published 2013 by Left Coast Press, Inc.

Published 2016 by Routledge
2 Park Square, Milton Park, Abingdon, Oxon OX14 4RN
711 Third Avenue, New York, NY 10017, USA

Routledge is an imprint of the Taylor & Francis Group, an informa business

Copyright © 2013 Taylor & Francis

All rights reserved. No part of this book may be reprinted or reproduced or utilised in any form or by any electronic, mechanical, or other means, now known or hereafter invented, including photocopying and recording, or in any information storage or retrieval system, without permission in writing from the publishers.

Notice:
Product or corporate names may be trademarks or registered trademarks, and are used only for identification and explanation without intent to infringe.

Library of Congress Cataloging-in-Publication Data

Galman, Sally Campbell.
  The good, the bad, and the data : Shane the Lone ethnographer's basic guide to qualitative data analysis.
    pages cm
  ISBN 978-1-59874-632-7 (pbk. : alk. paper) -- ISBN 978-1-61132-710-6
  1. Ethnology--Research. 2. Ethnology--Fieldwork. 3. Ethnology--Methodology. I. Title.
  GN345.G34 2013
  305.80072--dc23
                              2013012568

ISBN 978-1-59874-632-7 paperback

Table of Contents

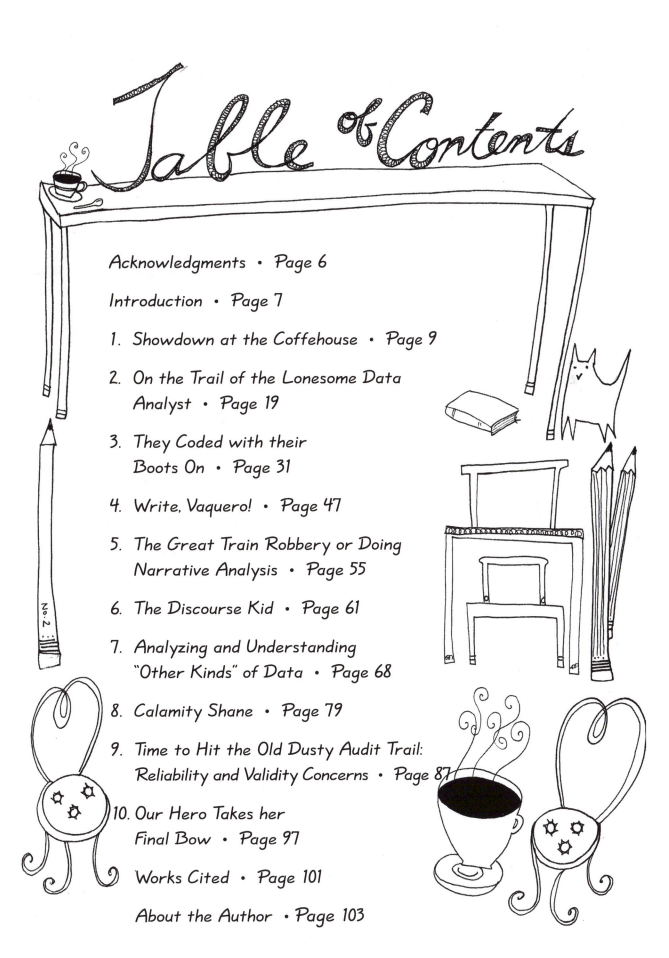

ACKNOWLEDGMENTS

This book would not have been possible without kindness, support and hard-working help from so many people. To name just a few:

☆ Kysa Nygreen, Christine Mallozzi, Jeanine Staples, Melisa Cahnmann-Taylor, Katrina Daly Thompson and Florence Sullivan, who contributed their professional expertise AND let me try to draw them and then publish my imperfect versions of their likenesses.

☆ My funny, delightful and oh-so-patient editor, Mitch Allen. Mitch knows that drawing is hard work, that erasing is even harder, and he can even help you with a chapter heading or gag when you are stuck stuck stuck.

☆ The anonymous reviewers who read the early drafts. Thank you, whoever you are, for your brilliant advice and gentle critique. Your help focused and improved the book, and my thinking.

☆ Professor Margaret LeCompte, who told me I should really bring my art into my scholarship.

☆ Professor Ernie Washington, who convinced a tenure and promotion committee that art *is* scholarship.

☆ The students in my many semesters of EDUC 797A, "Qualitative Data Analysis," who were subjected to connecting the dots, sorting toys and exploding pies.

☆ My husband Matt, who did the extra pick up and drop off and dinners and potty training and baths and homework with all our little kids because "Mommy has to draw tonight."

☆ Mother and Daddy, who always cheered me on.

☆ The original Sanjay, you know who you are.

INTRODUCTION

Dear Reader,

Welcome! Most people do not bother to read the introduction to a comic book so you are already ahead of the game. I hope you are ready to catch up with Shane, who has been busily watching movies and drinking coffee since the publication of this book's companion volume, *Shane the Lone Ethnographer* in 2007. She is still the same Shane—graduate student, qualitative researcher, Western film buff, and procrastinator extraordinaire. That it took six years for her to get from data collection to analysis should be a surprise to no one.

I'll bet you want to know…

How is Shane still in graduate school after all these years?

Yes, Shane is still in graduate school. One might say she is not making meteoric progress. She spends more time at Le Chat Furieux than she does at her studies and, alas for Shane, she may not graduate on schedule. In the first book we watch Shane as she navigates study design and begins to understand the relationship between ethnographic research, theory, and fieldcraft. She manages to complete her first ethnography and even dips her toes into the murky waters of data analysis and writing. However, it is only in this volume that she gets into qualitative data analysis in a more in-depth and operationalized fashion. She certainly takes her time. This is good news for us, as it is through her struggles and from her mistakes that we might learn.

In this volume we find Shane scrambling to relearn the entire contents of her qualitative data analysis course taken a few years ago when she was an enthusiastic masters student in order to be competitive for an assistantship. We will see what happens with that.

What do all the cowboy hats, campfires, and cattle have to do with qualitative research? I am confused. Isn't that the animal husbandry department?

Well, you're no fun. Where is your sense of whimsy? Yes, this book is about qualitative data analysis, just as the first book, *Shane the Lone Ethnographer*, was about setting up study design, uses of theory, and data collection methods . You will notice that both texts have a certain Wild West theme, hence all those people in cowboy hats. In this volume, which follows Shane from where Lone Ethnographer left off, readers will come to understand qualitative data analysis through the fanciful lens of the Wild West film genre. Readers will learn about narrative analysis by examining a train robbery and will enjoy chapters that evoke the mysteries of the proverbial dusty trail. There are some parallels between QDA and riding off into the sunset to explore the unknown. Even our heroine's name is taken from a classic Western film. I've taken some liberties (the movie posters in the opening pages featuring titles like *Squat Man* and *3:10 to Yucca* are obvious plays on original film titles because we can't just copy things willy nilly now can we?) but the overall gist is there and is intended to provide some universal case material for understanding complex ideas. As in data analysis, it is always good to have an organizing metaphor. In fact, if you pay careful attention there are no fewer than 23 references to classic Western films in this book—see if you can find them all. While there is no prize if you succeed, I can guarantee you a feeling of smug self-satisfaction that will last until the chuckwagon bell rings.

Isn't qualitative data analysis more complex than this? I mean, this is a comic book for crying out loud!

Yes, this is in fact a comic book. The pictures are a dead giveaway. Further, I agree with you: qualitative data analysis IS complex, much more complex than I can present here. Data analysis is a cognitive and theoretical task; there are simply loads of books that address the theoretical underpinnings and complex cognitive processes that make up much of the work of data analysis. In fact, I've included many of them in the Further Reading section at the back of this book. However, what these books don't offer is a concrete guide for what to do when you sit down to begin. Therefore, this text errs on the side of the pragmatic: it is a basic guide aimed at students and other beginners who have lots of ideas but need help with getting started. The use of the "cookbook" approach—meaning, putting concrete procedural knowledge out there—is meant to provide a basic how-to in approachable

shorthand, but also hinting at the deeper, richer work afoot within and behind those processes. This book is a general introduction but it does contain all the content needed to direct a basic, novice QDA project—and the schema provided can help any reader embark on further learning. The idea of a "cookbook" comes from my admonition to my own doctoral students, whom I exhort to be profoundly mechanical in their methodological write-ups. I tell them that someone should be able to read their methods sections and know how to reproduce their studies, as one might read a cookbook. Further, I like the idea of producing a "cookbook" from this text. Shane searches for her own cookbook-cum-cribnotes as a jumping-off place for the beginner. To wit: every cook needs to start somewhere, and sometimes it is easier for a beginner to set out to make a tin of muffins than to create a ten-tier fondant cake with buttercream filling topped with a marzipan replica of Neuschwanstein castle. If you want to become a professional baker, then you will eventually need to learn much more. But that all comes with time, study, and practice. This book is a good place to start learning to bake that first tin of muffins. I tell my students that data analysis seems scary at first, but will be tremendous fun once you get the basics down.

I promise you that this is true.

So, saddle up and start reading.

Fondly,

Sally *(and Shane)*

For more about study design, theoretical frames and data collection—as well as tantalizing Shane back-story—do read the companion volume (Galman 2007). This book simply picks up where that one left off. And did I mention that it is a fantastic read?

Chapter One
SHOWDOWN
AT THE COFFEEHOUSE

Sally Campbell Galman, "Showdown at the Coffeehouse," in *The Good, the Bad, and the Data: Shane the Lone Ethnographer's Basic Guide to Qualitative Data Analysis*, pp. 9-18. © 2013 Left Coast Press, Inc. All rights reserved.

WHILE SHANE'S OUT SEARCHING, WE ARE GOING TO TAKE A MINUTE TO HEAR FROM AN EXPERT IN THE FIELD. WE ASKED DR. KYSA NYGREEN,

HOW DO YOU GET STARTED WITH DATA ANALYSIS?

SMARTY PANTS TIPS N°1

MEET DR. NYGREEN, AUTHOR OF THESE KIDS: AN ETHNO-GRAPHY OF ALTERNATIVE HIGH SCHOOL STUDENTS (U. CHICAGO PRESS).

SHE'S A REAL EXPERT ON GETTING STARTED!

MOO?

DATA

"THE FIRST THING I DO IS TAKE STOCK OF WHAT I HAVE (AND, IDEALLY, I HAVE BEEN DOING THAT ALL ALONG)"

NOT THAT KIND OF STOCK!

"TAKING STOCK MEANS..."

FIRST I GO TO MY COMPUTER AND LOOK AT ALL MY DATA, WHICH I ORGANIZED INTO FILE FOLDERS TO BEGIN WITH.

I HAVE A FOLDER FOR:
AUDIO FILES
TRANSCRIPTS
FIELDNOTES
ARTIFACTS
MEMOS,
ETC.

I ALSO SCAN ANY HARD COPY STUFF.

hard copy

I OPEN EACH FOLDER AND I MAKE THIS GIANT LIST OF ALL MY FILES AND HARD COPY.

THIS LIST IS MY DATA MATRIX. I TYPE IT INTO EXCEL SO I CAN KEEP TRACK OF WHAT I DO IN COLUMNS — LIKE WHAT I HAVE TRANSCRIBED AND WHAT STILL NEEDS WORK.

	A	B	C	D	E	F	G	H	
1	AUDIO FILES & TRANSCRIPTION								
2									
3	File name	What it is	Length	Format	Language	Transcribed?	Priority	Order	COMMENTS
4									
48	2009 10-16 Audio field notes by K	field notes	1:31	mp3	E	N	n/a		do not transcribe
49	2009 10-16 Audio field notes by K	field notes	1:31:52	mp3	E	N	n/a		do not transcribe
50	2009 10-17 Audio field notes by K	field notes	7:59	mp3	E	N	n/a		do not transcribe
51	2009 10-17 Audio field notes by K	field notes	16:47	mp3	E	N	n/a		do not transcribe
52	2010 4-2 Eval Workshop (G) #1	staff mtg	2:00	mp3	E	R	L		
53	2010 4-2 Eval Workshop (G) #2	staff mtg	1:27:44	mp3	E	R	L		
	2010 3-17 205X	interview	1:09:52	mp3	E	N	H	21	
	2010 3-19 H#1	interview	47:58:00	mp3	E	N	H	19	
	2010 3-19 H#2	reflection on in	8:45	mp3	E	N	n/a		do not transcribe
	2010 4-5 L	interview	40:03:00	mp3	E	R	L		
	2010 4-5 T	interview	1:23:43	mp3	E	R	L		
	2010 4-7 T	interview	1:19:36	mp3	E	R	L		
	2010 4-7 012X	interview	46:40:00	mp3	E	R	L		
	2010 3-10 X012 Interview	interview	1:06:27	mp3	E	N	M		
	2010 3-11 Regeneracion focus grou	staff mtg	20:21:00	mp3	E	N	M		
	2010 3-11 X102 Interview	interview	57:20:00	mp3	E	N	M		
	2010 3-13 X023 Interview	interview	1:00:42	mp3	E	N	M		
	2010 3-14 X048 Interview	interview	56:29:00	mp3	E	N	M		
	2010 3-14 madres	interview	20:20	mp3	S	N	H	20	
	2010 3-14 Audio field notes	field notes	8:42	mp3	E	N	n/a		do not transcribe
	2010 3-16 323X Interview	interview	54:09:00	mp3	E	N	M		

NAMES ARE CODES FOR DATE, PLACE, PERSON OR GROUP.

THEN I MAKE A PLAN. I PRETTY MUCH START READING BY DATE.

I READ AND READ AND READ AND TAKE NOTES IN THE MARGINS.

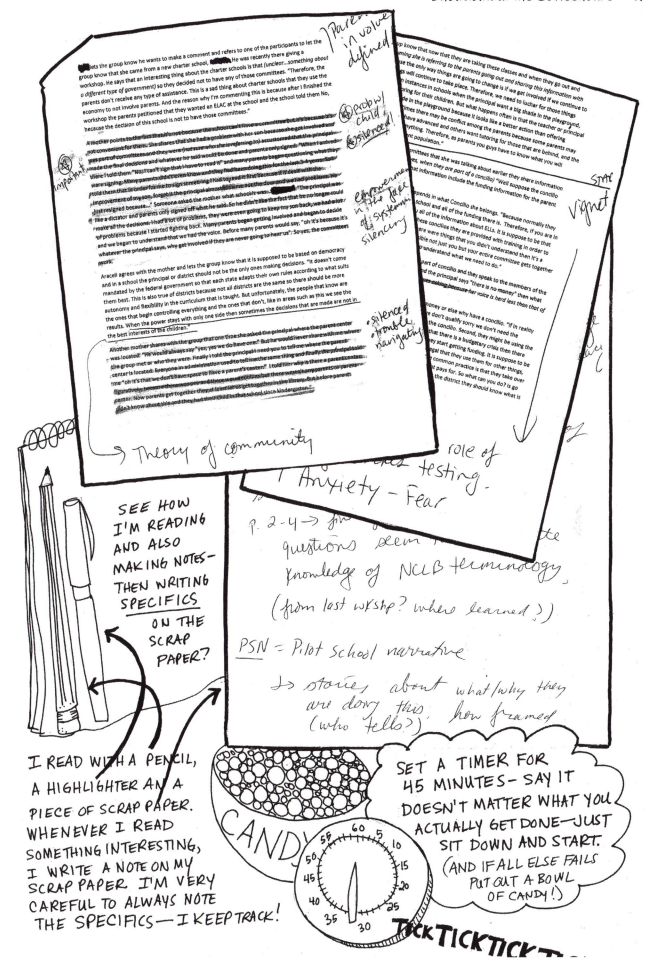

REMEMBER:

WHAT WE NAME OUR "BUCKETS" IS VERY IMPORTANT.

IT HAS A DIRECT IMPACT ON THE RESULTS OF ANALYSIS.

STUFF THAT HAS BEEN CHEWED

SO, USING INDUCTIVE AND DEDUCTIVE STRATEGIES HELPS MAKE GOOD "BUCKETS"

we were interested in blocks.

where does THIS go?

IT LOOKS LIKE WE HAVE A LOT OF SMILEY BLOCKS — LET'S MAKE A BUCKET.

GROUNDED THEORY

by Strauss & Corbin & Glaser...

PEOPLE WHO FRAME THEIR WORK USING <u>GROUNDED THEORY</u> DEVELOP THEORY USING A COMPLEX BOTTOM-UP, OR <u>INDUCTIVE</u> PROCESS.

(TYPICALLY, ETHNOGRAPHERS AND OTHERS USE TOP-DOWN AND BOTTOM-UP <u>BOTH</u>)

BUT DON'T JUST TAKE IT FROM ME — LET'S ASK AN EXPERT!

MOO

- - - - - CUT HERE TO ADD TO YOUR COOKBOOK - - - - -

I GOT IT! ANOTHER PAGE OF THE COOKBOOK OF THE SIERRA MADRES!

WHAT IS YOUR ORGANIZING METAPHOR FOR DATA ANALYSIS? IS YOUR WORK PRIMARILY <u>INDUCTIVE</u> OR <u>DEDUCTIVE</u>?

SMARTY PANTS TIP No. 2

? ? ? ? ? ? ? ? ?

SHE SAYS: "I AM OFTEN <u>SWIMMING</u> IN DATA ABOUT WHAT IT MEANS TO ATTEND U.S. INSTITUTIONS OF EDUCATION AS SOMEONE WHO IS POOR AND WHO SPEAKS A NON-ENGLISH LANGUAGE AT HOME

DR. CAHNMANN-TAYLOR IS A PROFESSOR WHO STUDIES

LANGUAGE & POWER

POET AND SCHOLAR EXTRAORDINAIRE

MEET DR. MELISA CAHNMANN-TAYLOR

"... It is when fundamental and unexamined assumptions of mind and nature are shaken that we are most moved, in the arts as in science... The most profound discoveries—those described as REVOLUTIONARY or 'EARTH-SHAKING' - are ones, like the Copernican rearrangement of sun and planets, that REVISE OUR MOST DAILY, UNQUESTIONED ASSUMPTIONS."

to illustrate this SURPRISE I share two pieces of the same data — coded by two different researchers:

1   2

we are studying poem - drafts of several international Chinese students— to analyze their English language development and emergence of social critique through the creative writing process.

#1
You are the journey I'd like to take,

the waterfall is your neatly combed hair,

a splash of water over the naked rock,

[just like a pearl embedded in your hairpin.]

ORIGINAL, SENSUOUS IMAGERY

KAPOW! + HIGHLY ORIGINAL USE OF METAPHOR

Under the [willow-leaf eyebrow] are your leaping

eyelashes, twinkling like the dancing reeds in the breeze,

along with [circumocular crinkle,] ———— NNS-DICTION

ripple and melt away in your [watery-misted eyes.]

KAPOW! + ORIGINAL WAY TO SAY "TEARS" CONNECTED TO WATERFALL IMAGE ABOVE

The first coding was done by myself where I largely respond to what appears to be the development of original and surprising metaphors for describing the beloved.

The SURPRISE came when my collaborator, a Chinese - English bilingual graduate student, observed that many of the metaphors I identified as "fresh" were actually translations of cliché language use in Chinese!

This kind of inductive noticing led to a research team discussion about missed opportunities in the TESOL classroom.

#2
You are the journey I'd like to take,

[the waterfall is your neatly combed hair,]

a splash of water over the naked rock,

just like a pearl embedded in your hairpin.

cliché

HOME - CULTURE: A TYPICAL METAPHOR FOR A LADY'S EYE-BROW IN CHINESE

Under the [willow-leaf eyebrow] are your leaping

eyelashes, twinkling like the dancing [reeds] in the breeze,

along with circumocular crinkle,

ripple and melt away in your watery-misted eyes.

L POPULAR IMAGE IN CHINESE POETRY

SADDLE UP! IT'S...

HOMEWORK NUMBER **2** THE "BUCKET LIST"

IN OUR LAST HOMEWORK EXERCISE, YOU TIDIED UP YOUR DATA TO BEGIN READING.

NOW YOU ARE GOING TO THINK DEEPLY ABOUT YOUR DEDUCTIVE BUCKETS.

REMEMBER THAT YOU HAVEN'T BEGUN TO EXPLODE YOUR DATA YET...

Yummy

SO WE AREN'T IN THE BUSINESS OF INDUCTIVE BUCKETS YET.

SMILEY BLOCK

WE MAKE OUR **DEDUCTIVE** BUCKETS BY THINKING ABOUT OUR
① RESEARCH QUESTION
&
② CONCEPTUAL & THEORETICAL FRAMEWORKS

1. GO BACK TO YOUR RESEARCH QUESTION. WHAT ARE THE IMPORTANT BIG IDEAS IN IT? WRITE THEM DOWN ON THE LIST BELOW.

2. GO BACK TO YOUR THEORETICAL AND CONCEPTUAL FRAMEWORKS. PULL OUT THE BIG IDEAS. PUT THEM ON THE LIST TOO.

3. NOW, LABEL SOME BUCKETS. USE THE ONES BELOW AND DRAW MORE IF YOU NEED TO. YOU CAN ALSO MAKE REAL ONES OUT OF CUPS OR PAPER.

4. ON INDEX CARDS, WRITE OUT SOME SHORT DESCRIPTIONS OF WHAT KINDS OF THINGS YOU EXPECT TO PUT IN EACH BUCKET.

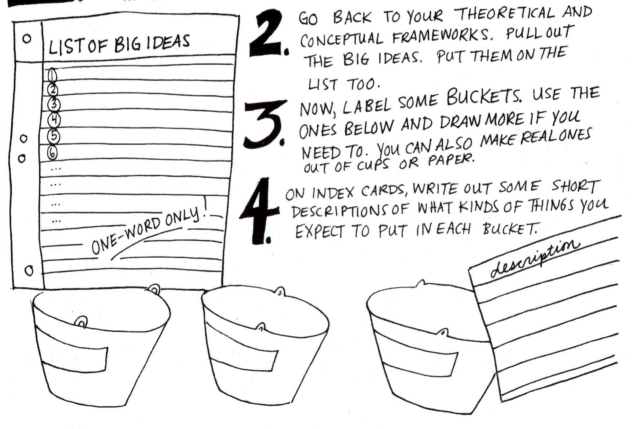

LIST OF BIG IDEAS
① ② ③ ④ ⑤ ⑥ ... ...
ONE-WORD ONLY!

description

Sally Campbell Galman, "They Coded With Their Boots On," in *The Good, the Bad, and the Data: Shane the Lone Ethnographer's Basic Guide to Qualitative Data Analysis*, pp. 31-46. © 2013 Left Coast Press, Inc. All rights reserved.

BUT HOW DO I CHOOSE WHAT TO CALL MY CODES?

NAMING THE "BUCKETS" IS EASY, BUT HOW DO I MAKE NOTES IN THE ACTUAL DATA?

SOME CODES ARE EASIER TO USE THAN OTHERS.

WHAT DID "XITTP4Q" MEAN?

A GOOD CODE IS MEANINGFUL, AND HAS CORRESPONDENCE TO ACTUAL IDEAS.

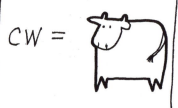

CW =

LECOMPTE & SCHENSUL CALL THIS A "LOW LEVEL OF INFERENCE" (p. 57, 1999)

BT =

THIS MEANS THAT YOU USE WORDS OR ABBREVIATIONS THAT ARE VERY CLOSE TO THE MEANING OF WHAT YOU ARE CODING FOR.

YOU ALSO DON'T WANT HUGE PHRASES AS CODES—KEEP IT SHORT. AND DON'T MAKE CRAZY ABBREVIATIONS— THINGS SHOULD MAKE QUICK SENSE.

CWBYHA =

LET'S IMAGINE A STUDY OF STAGECOACH ROBBERS' PREFERRED METHODS.

YOU KNOW THAT ONE "DEDUCTIVE BUCKET" MIGHT BE THE IDEA OF ROBBERY.

A GOOD CODE MIGHT BE

AND YOU ARE ALSO INTERESTED IN THE BANDITS' USE OF MASKS.

SO...

AND, AS YOU READ, YOU ALSO FIND THE BANDITS GREW BUSHY MUSTACHES.

SO, YOU NEED ANOTHER CODE—

AND THEN, READING ON, YOU FIND THAT BANDITS ALSO TERRIFIED STAGECOACH PASSENGERS BY WAVING GIANT TROUT.*

EEEK! A TROUT!

YOU GET THE IDEA.

* OKAY. JUST KIDDING ABOUT THE TROUT.

SO, AFTER A WHILE OF READING THROUGH YOUR DATA, LOOKING TO FILL DEDUCTIVE BUCKETS _AND_ NEW INDUCTIVE BUCKETS THAT SPRING UP...

...YOU WILL HAVE A NICE BIG LIST OF CODES. SO NICE!

THEY ARE MEANINGFUL. THEY ARE LOW-INFERENCE. THEY CONNECT WITH YOUR BUCKETS.

YOU FEEL GOOD WHEN YOU USE THEM.

MAYBE YOU HAVE A FRIEND OR COLLEAGUE WHO WANTS TO HELP YOU CODE YOUR DATA!

help is good!

HOW DO YOU KEEP TRACK OF YOUR CODES, USE THEM CONSISTENTLY, AND GET OTHERS TO ALSO USE THEM?

ANSWER:

YOU PUT THEM IN A BOOK

THE CODEBOOK.

A CODEBOOK IS YOUR FINAL LIST OF CODES, WITH DETAILED INFORMATION OF WHAT THEY MEAN, AND HOW THEY WILL APPEAR IN THE DATA.

IMPORTANT TERM! ↘ WHEN YOU DEFINE A CONCEPT IN SUCH A WAY AS TO "KNOW IT" CLEARLY WHEN YOU "SEE IT" YOU ARE OPERATIONALIZING SAID CONCEPT.

FOR EXAMPLE...

WE CAN THINK ABOUT THE LITTLE-KNOWN BUT VERY EXCITING WESTERN FILM:

THE CODEBOOK OF

Zorro

BECAUSE DOING DATA ANALYSIS IN THE OLD WEST REQUIRES THE WHOLE ALPHABET.

EN-GARDE!

FOR A WHILE, ZORRO WAS ONLY CODING WITH THE LETTER Z

THIS MADE CODING HIS QUALITATIVE DATA VERY DIFFICULT

The alcalde stole all of our cows and then made us buy them back from him. What a jerk. Somebody ought to teach him a lesson already. I mean, we have democracy here, don't we? Can't we vote him out. Uh, wait—I think so. Can you check on

WHAT DO ALL THESE Z's MEAN?

CODEBOOK

THEORY

GROUND

We TALKED A LITTLE BIT ABOUT GROUNDED THEORY EARLIER, BUT IT'S A NICE WAY TO THINK DEEPLY ABOUT CODING, AND WHAT YOU CAN DO WITH YOUR CODES— SO, HERE WE GO AGAIN!

GROUNDED THEORY AFFIRMS THAT THE TOP-DOWN ANALYTIC APPROACH NEED NOT BE THE ONLY ONE. THEORY CAN ALSO COME FROM AN INDUCTIVE, "BOTTOM-UP" APPROACH.

STRAUSS & CORBIN (1998) SAY IT BEST:

Grounded theory is "theory derived from data, systematically gathered, and analyzed . . . in this method, data collection, analysis and eventual theory stand in close relationship to one another . . . the researcher begins with an area of study and allows the theory to emerge from the data."

SO, GROUNDED THEORY IS MORE THAN JUST PROCEDURAL. IT IS A WAY OF THINKING ABOUT THEORY AND THE WORLD!

IT'S IMPORTANT TO THINK ABOUT WHILE WE CODE BECAUSE:

1. IT'S FUN TO THINK ABOUT AN WHOLLY INDUCTIVE PROCESS.

2. THE PROCESS OF CODING IS ESPECIALLY INTENSIVE IN THE GROUNDED THEORY UNIVERSE.

3. LEARNING TO CODE IN THE GROUNDED THEORY WAY IS GREAT FOR DEVELOPING YOUR SKILLS, WHETHER YOU WANT TO ULTIMATELY "DO" G.T. OR NOT.

THE G.T. BASICS!

⇒ GO THROUGH YOUR DATA, NOTING CONCEPTS, "OPENING UP" THE DATA.

⇒ CLUMP YOUR CONCEPTS TOGETHER TO MAKE RELATED GROUPS. THESE ARE CALLED "CATEGORIES"

⇒ PUT THOSE CATEGORIES TOGETHER TO MAKE A STORY ABOUT WHAT IS GOING ON IN YOUR DATA.

⇒ GIVE YOUR STORY A NAME.

REMEMBER, AT ITS MOST BASIC, A THEORY IS A STORY

INDUCTIVE BUCKET

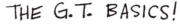

THE FIRST STEP, "OPENING UP" THE DATA, IS CALLED OPEN CODING.

WHEN YOU OPEN CODE YOU ARE LOOKING AT PIECES (WORDS, LINES, PARAGRAPHS, PAGES) AND MINING THEM FOR CONCEPTS.

IT CAN BE VERY TIME-CONSUMING

IT'S A LITTLE BIT LIKE HOW WE "EXPLODED" THE DATA IN CHAPTER 2.

AND YOU NEED TO BE PRECISE.

HERE'S AN EXAMPLE OF SOME DATA THAT HAS BEEN OPEN CODED.

HERE AT THE BEGINNING WE SEE A LOT OF WORD-BY-WORD, ALMOST MICROSCOPIC CODING, WHERE THE FOCUS IS ON WORDS AND ON THEIR MEANING

```
1  Bob: At first I wasn't sure I had a lot of moles in
2  the yard but then I could see all the little wriggly
3  dirt lines all over the place . . . (for real it was a
4  huge mess like you'd walk four feet and all of a
5  sudden you would be up to your ankles in the
6  dirt. And forget about grass growing because
7  you know they kill everything. But aren't they
8  also aerating the yard?
9  Jim: Aerating? I have worms for that. I mean,
10 are they at least eating the slugs?
11 Bob: I don't know. I think they eat grubs.
12 Jim: What is the difference between a slug and
13 a grub? They both sound gross.
14 Bob: Yeah I think they are both pretty gross.
15 Jim: Do you think we can fish with them?
16 Bob: Most gross things make pretty good bait.
17 Jim: Right. Like nightcrawlers—those worm
18 things, what are they called?
19 Bob: I don't know. Worms are gross. That's why
20 I don't fish.
21 Jim: Yeah. Do moles eat worms?
22 Bob: Probably.
23 Jim: You know, they are actually kind of cute. All
24 velvety and soft.
25 Bob: What? Those are the things destroying my
26 lawn! What are you talking about?
27 Jim: Well I dunno, they are pretty cute. I mean,
28 I saw one once and I wanted to pick it up and
29 give it a little stroke. Just to see how soft it was.
30 Bob: Well, when I get them out of my yard you
31 can keep them all.
32 Jim: I read once that in England they have these
33 guys who will come to your house and sing a
34 special song to the moles to get them to leave
35 your yard. They sing the song, and all the moles
36 are, like, hypnotized and come out of their
37 holes. Or something like that. These guys are
38 even unionized. They have some sort of Royal
39 Order of the British Molecatcher.
40 Bob: They take that stuff really seriously over
41 there.
```

sub-terranean creature
adj- creative/natural observ.
locator (non-specific)
qualifier (emphasis)
soil ref.
violence ref.] neg = moles
creatures
purported function of moles
constructing knowledge
qual
creatures
second purpose
creatures
qual.
functionalities of moles
pos. attributes mole
violence
rhet. (qualifier)
uncertainty
pos. mole
sarc.
historical; narrative/story
coda

NOTE: GROUNDED THEORISTS OFTEN STRIVE TO USE ONE-WORD DESCRIPTORS. THIS RESEARCHER USES SOME, BUT WILL NEED TO CLEAN UP SOME OTHER ONES LATER.

THIS RESEARCHER MIGHT WANT TO DOUBLE-SPACE OR USE HIGHLIGHTERS FOR CLARITY.

HERE WE SEE MORE LINE-BY-LINE AND PARAGRAPH-LEVEL CODING.

NUMBERING YOUR LINES IS A GREAT IDEA BECAUSE YOU CAN REFERENCE LINES.

NOW, LET'S SAY THIS RESEARCHER IS CODING ALONG AND HAS AN IMPORTANT IDEA OR EVEN MAKES A CONNECTION TO SOMETHING AND THERE'S ONLY SO MUCH ROOM IN THE MARGIN...

SHE WRITES A MEMO!

Memo

I've noticed that there is a real juxtapositioning between "bad" wildlife [things that are "gross" or that "kill" plants and cause problems] and "cute" or "good" wildlife [as Jim positions the mole]. Can the mole occupy both positions but under different conditions?

YOU CAN WRITE LOTS OF MEMOS!

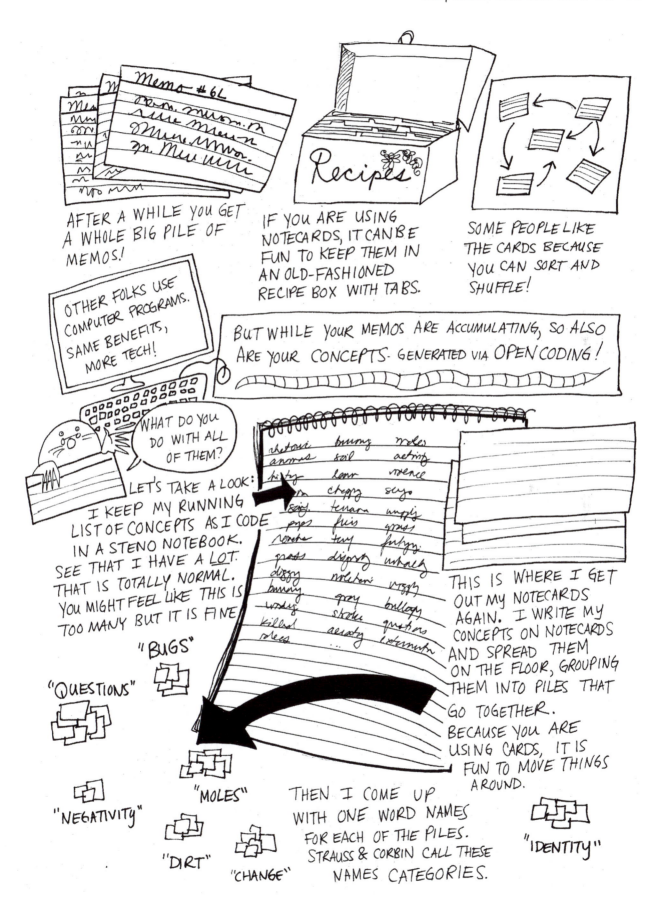

AFTER A WHILE YOU GET A WHOLE BIG PILE OF MEMOS!

IF YOU ARE USING NOTECARDS, IT CAN BE FUN TO KEEP THEM IN AN OLD-FASHIONED RECIPE BOX WITH TABS.

SOME PEOPLE LIKE THE CARDS BECAUSE YOU CAN SORT AND SHUFFLE!

OTHER FOLKS USE COMPUTER PROGRAMS. SAME BENEFITS, MORE TECH!

BUT WHILE YOUR MEMOS ARE ACCUMULATING, SO ALSO ARE YOUR CONCEPTS - GENERATED VIA OPEN CODING!

WHAT DO YOU DO WITH ALL OF THEM?

LET'S TAKE A LOOK: I KEEP MY RUNNING LIST OF CONCEPTS AS I CODE IN A STENO NOTEBOOK. SEE THAT I HAVE A LOT. THAT IS TOTALLY NORMAL. YOU MIGHT FEEL LIKE THIS IS TOO MANY BUT IT IS FINE.

THIS IS WHERE I GET OUT MY NOTECARDS AGAIN. I WRITE MY CONCEPTS ON NOTECARDS AND SPREAD THEM ON THE FLOOR, GROUPING THEM INTO PILES THAT GO TOGETHER. BECAUSE YOU ARE USING CARDS, IT IS FUN TO MOVE THINGS AROUND.

"BUGS"

"QUESTIONS"

"NEGATIVITY"

"MOLES"

"DIRT"

"CHANGE"

THEN I COME UP WITH ONE WORD NAMES FOR EACH OF THE PILES. STRAUSS & CORBIN CALL THESE NAMES CATEGORIES.

"IDENTITY"

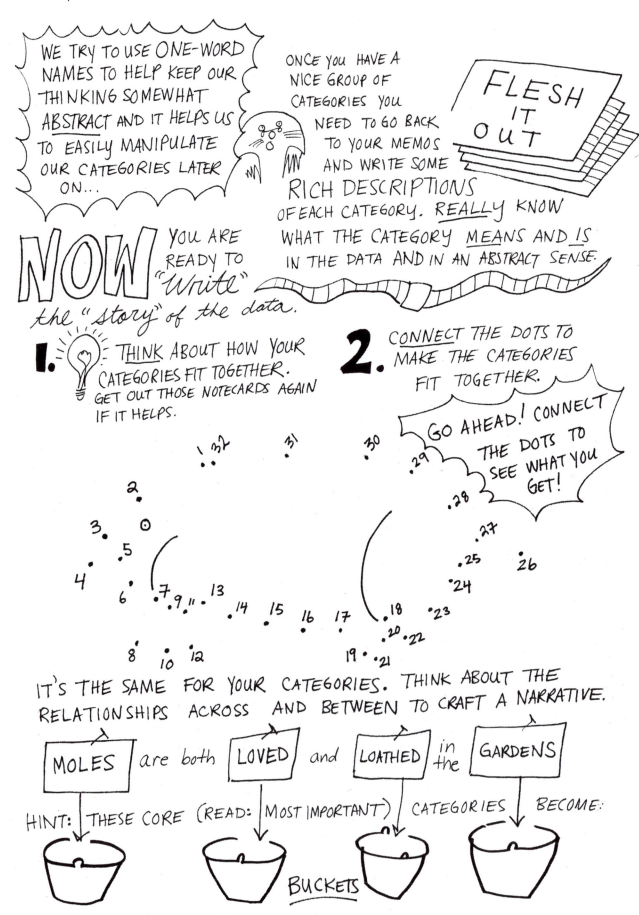

WE TRY TO USE ONE-WORD NAMES TO HELP KEEP OUR THINKING SOMEWHAT ABSTRACT AND IT HELPS US TO EASILY MANIPULATE OUR CATEGORIES LATER ON...

ONCE YOU HAVE A NICE GROUP OF CATEGORIES YOU NEED TO GO BACK TO YOUR MEMOS AND WRITE SOME RICH DESCRIPTIONS OF EACH CATEGORY. REALLY KNOW WHAT THE CATEGORY MEANS AND IS IN THE DATA AND IN AN ABSTRACT SENSE.

FLESH IT OUT

NOW YOU ARE READY TO "Write" the "story" of the data.

1. THINK ABOUT HOW YOUR CATEGORIES FIT TOGETHER. GET OUT THOSE NOTECARDS AGAIN IF IT HELPS.

2. CONNECT THE DOTS TO MAKE THE CATEGORIES FIT TOGETHER.

GO AHEAD! CONNECT THE DOTS TO SEE WHAT YOU GET!

IT'S THE SAME FOR YOUR CATEGORIES. THINK ABOUT THE RELATIONSHIPS ACROSS AND BETWEEN TO CRAFT A NARRATIVE.

MOLES are both LOVED and LOATHED in the GARDENS

HINT: THESE CORE (READ: MOST IMPORTANT) CATEGORIES BECOME:

BUCKETS

then we tried to apply those codes to the rest of the cases, looking at what worked, and what didn't.

code
↳ category
↓
properties

We also came up with categories, and properties.

The bold entries are the categories and under those are the properties. After this, we named the code and gave the code an operational description.

COMPOSING TEXT	
1. RISK TAKING: Takes risks with word meanings, spelling, and genres.	
2: WRITING WITH INTENT: Writes with an audience and purpose in mind.	
3: REVISION: Revises at the word and composition level.	
4: APPLICATION OF INSTRUCTION: Applies mini-lesson and strategies. [move to "working"?]	
5: AMBIGUITY: Tolerates uncertainty when drafting and revision compositions	
THINKING ABOUT WRITING	
6: WRITER'S LANGUAGE: Uses metalanguage to characterize words and the writing process.	
7: METACOGNITION: Reflects on word choice and language.	
WORKING ON WRITING	
8: STYLE: Chooses to work alone, with others, and at different paces.	
9. RESOURCES: Uses vocabulary resources to facilitate writing.	
USING VOCABULARY	
10: DICTION: Uses appropriate, inventive, and low-frequency words. [overuses, overgeneralizes words]	
11: HOT-WORD PHENOMENON: Adopts words that appear in multiple contexts.	

There were three of us on the project, so we needed to be VERY CLEAR about what each code was really about — we stuck with those codes.

And then, if things didn't fit into those codes, if things weren't useful, we revised them.

IN TERMS OF DOING CODING, HERE IS A PRELIMINARY ANALYSIS OF AN INTERVIEW. I TRANSCRIBED THE INTERVIEW AND PULLED OUT DIRECT QUOTATIONS THAT FIT THE THINGS I WAS LOOKING FOR IN THE STUDY.

I USE THREE COLUMNS:
- ONE FOR THE DIRECT QUOTES.
- ONE FOR THE PRELIMINARY ANALYSIS.
- ONE FOR MY OWN NOTES.

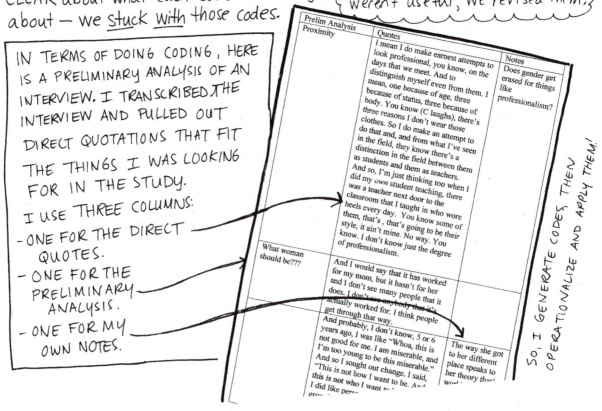

So, I GENERATE CODES, THEN OPERATIONALIZE AND APPLY THEM!

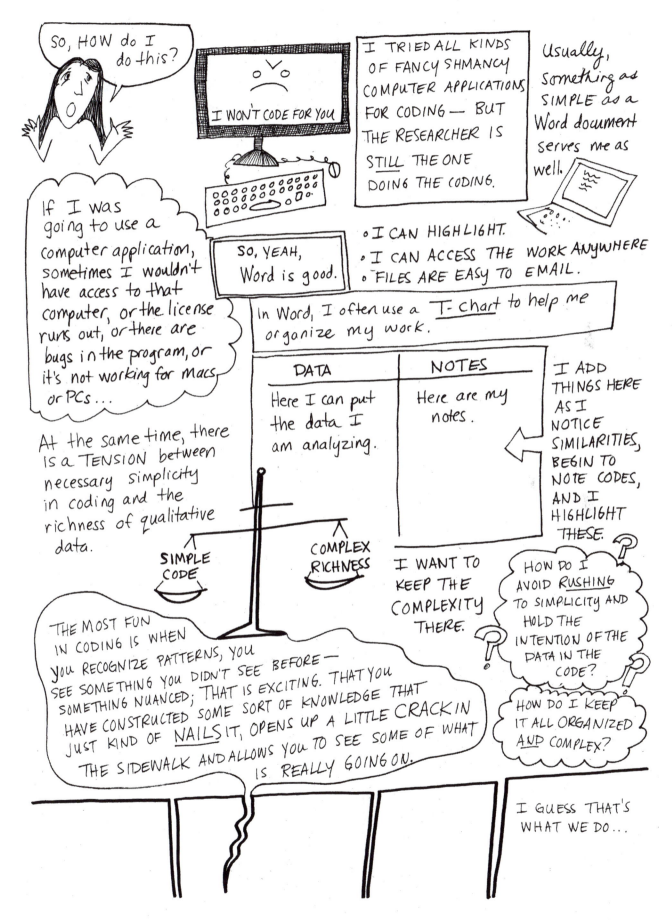

Homework #3

BZZZZ

IN HOMEWORK #1 YOU TIDIED UP & READ-THROUGH

IN HOMEWORK #2 YOU MADE DEDUCTIVE BUCKETS.

NOW WE WILL PRACTICE CODING & MAKE INDUCTIVE BUCKETS!

1. GO TO AN OFFICE SUPPLY STORE, BUY SOME DIFFERENT NOTEPADS, INDEX CARDS AND FUN PENS AND HIGHLIGHTERS.

2. PRACTICE THE OPEN CODING PROCESS. USE YOUR NEW STUFF!

BONUS CHALLENGE: TRY YOUR HAND AT WORD-BY-WORD, LINE-BY-LINE OR PARAGRAPH-LEVEL ANALYSIS.

3. MAKE AT LEAST 5 INDUCTIVE BUCKETS TO GO WITH YOUR 5 DEDUCTIVE BUCKETS.

USE YOUR CATEGORIES. TRY TO NOT THINK ABOUT YOUR DEDUCTIVE BUCKETS AND FOCUS ON INDUCTIVE THEMES.

4. MAKE A NICE LIST OF YOUR TEN BUCKETS. THEN OPERATIONALIZE EACH BUCKET LABEL AS A CODE. WRITE DOWN HOW YOU WILL KNOW EACH ONE WHEN YOU SEE IT IN THE DATA.

my first codebook

TA-DAH!

NOW GO BACK THROUGH YOUR DATA, NOTING THESE CODES!

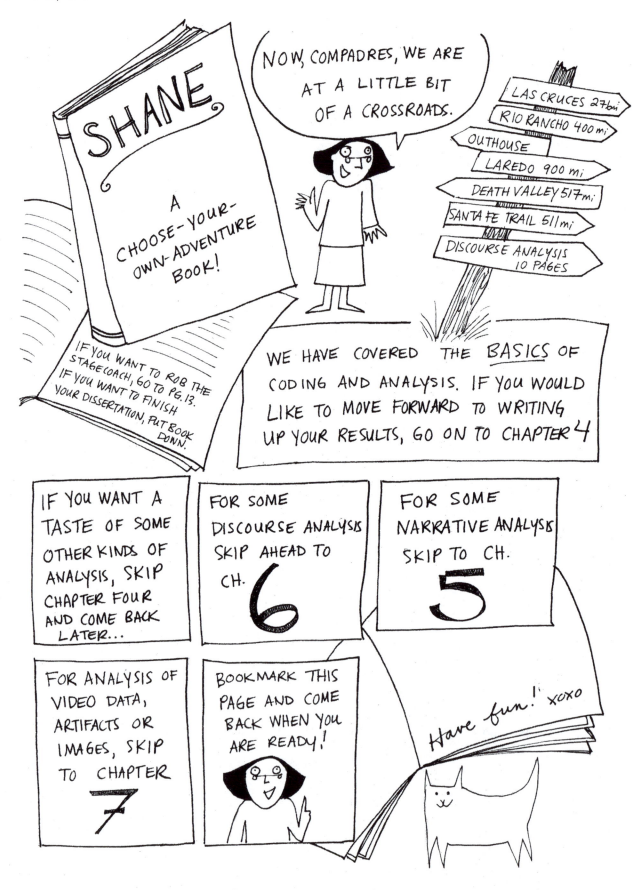

Sally Campbell Galman, "Write, Vaquero!," in *The Good, the Bad, and the Data: Shane the Lone Ethnographer's Basic Guide to Qualitative Data Analysis*, pp. 47-54. © 2013 Left Coast Press, Inc. All rights reserved.

OKAY. LET'S RECAP.

WAIT. I DID NOT SIGN UP TO BE A WRITER. I'M A *Researcher!*

THEN I HAVE SOME BAD NEWS FOR YOU.

"Qualitative researchers need to be storytellers . . . the ability to tell (which, in academia, essentially means to be able to write) a story well is crucial to the enterprise." Harry Wolcott (1994, p. 17)

BUT I'M A FIELD-WORKER! NOT A WRITER, A SCRIBBLER!

THE DATA SPEAKS FOR ITSELF!

TA-DA!

UH, NO. NOT QUITE

WRITING UP IS
★ TELLING THE STORY.
★ INTERPRETING THE STORY.
★ DISCUSSING THE RESULTS.
★ DESCRIBING ANALYTIC PROCEDURES.

WRITING UP IS A BIG PART OF THE WORK OF A RESEARCHER.

OKAY. F<u>I</u>NE.

REMEMBER ART AND SCIENCE?

HMPH.

OH, YOU'LL LOVE IT.

<u>FIRST</u> DO SOME THINKING ABOUT YOURSELF AS A WRITER. TAKE OUT A PIECE OF PAPER AND MAKE A LITTLE MEMO. WHAT KINDS OF WRITING HAVE YOU DONE? HOW DID YOU LEARN TO WRITE? WHAT DO YOU ENJOY ABOUT WRITING?

I REMEMBER THAT IN ELEMENTARY SCHOOL I WAS GIVEN <u>FRAMES</u>— LIKE GUIDELINES,

OR

I USED WEBS

TO ORGANIZE MY IDEAS.

THESE STRUCTURES WERE HELPFUL.

ACADEMIC WRITERS USE LOTS OF DIFFERENT FRAMES TO HELP THEM TOO. LET'S EXPLORE!

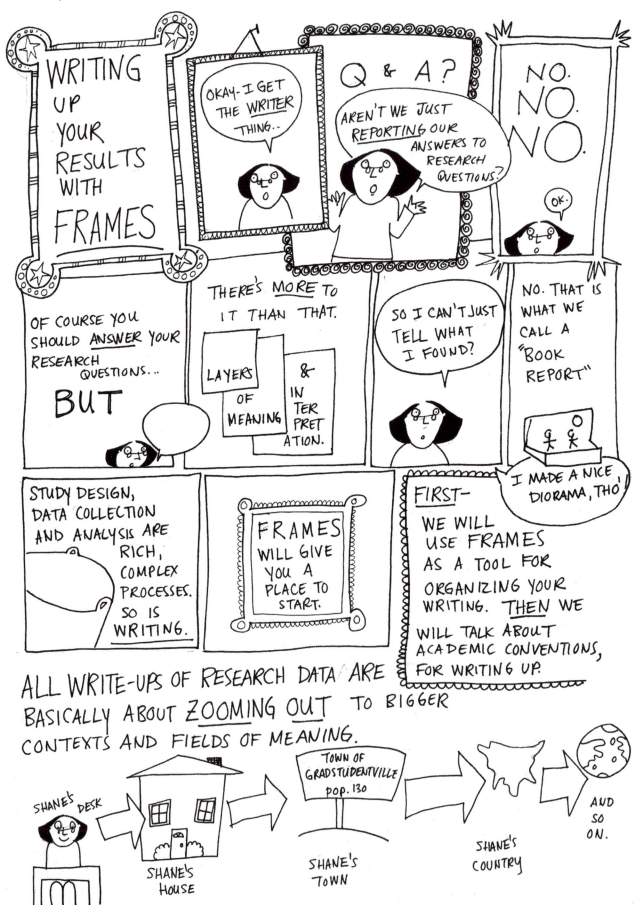

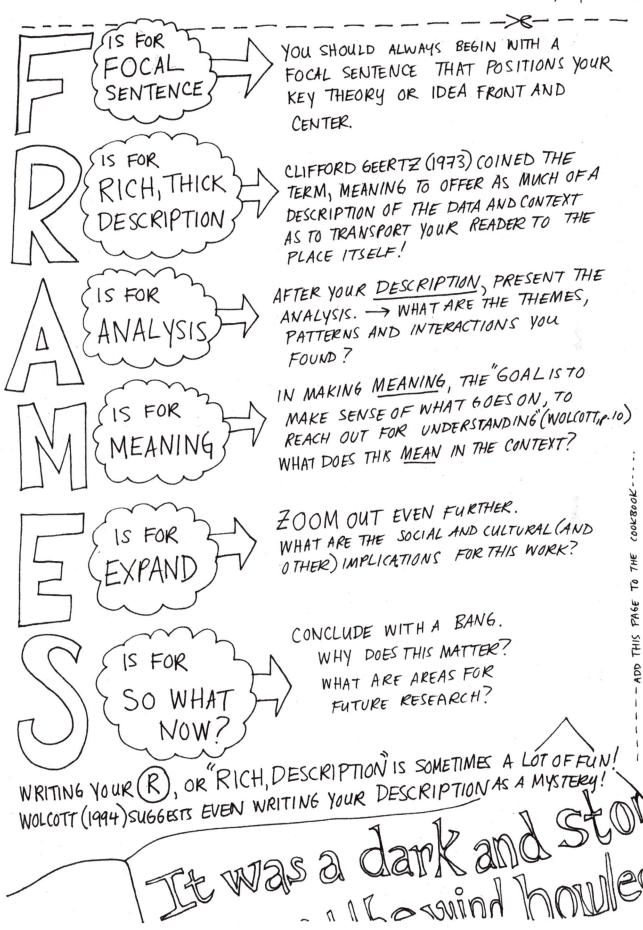

F IS FOR **FOCAL SENTENCE** → YOU SHOULD ALWAYS BEGIN WITH A FOCAL SENTENCE THAT POSITIONS YOUR KEY THEORY OR IDEA FRONT AND CENTER.

R IS FOR **RICH, THICK DESCRIPTION** → CLIFFORD GEERTZ (1973) COINED THE TERM, MEANING TO OFFER AS MUCH OF A DESCRIPTION OF THE DATA AND CONTEXT AS TO TRANSPORT YOUR READER TO THE PLACE ITSELF!

A IS FOR **ANALYSIS** → AFTER YOUR DESCRIPTION, PRESENT THE ANALYSIS. → WHAT ARE THE THEMES, PATTERNS AND INTERACTIONS YOU FOUND?

M IS FOR **MEANING** → IN MAKING MEANING, THE "GOAL IS TO MAKE SENSE OF WHAT GOES ON, TO REACH OUT FOR UNDERSTANDING" (WOLCOTT, p.10) WHAT DOES THIS MEAN IN THE CONTEXT?

E IS FOR **EXPAND** → ZOOM OUT EVEN FURTHER. WHAT ARE THE SOCIAL AND CULTURAL (AND OTHER) IMPLICATIONS FOR THIS WORK?

S IS FOR **SO WHAT NOW?** → CONCLUDE WITH A BANG. WHY DOES THIS MATTER? WHAT ARE AREAS FOR FUTURE RESEARCH?

-- -- ADD THIS PAGE TO THE COOKBOOK -- -- -

WRITING YOUR ⓡ, OR "RICH, DESCRIPTION" IS SOMETIMES A LOT OF FUN! WOLCOTT (1994) SUGGESTS EVEN WRITING YOUR DESCRIPTION AS A MYSTERY!

It was a dark and stor ...he wind howle

FOR EXAMPLE...

LET'S GO BACK TO CHAPTER 3... TO THE ZORRO STUDY.

FOR FUN, LET'S IMAGINE YOU ARE WRITING THIS STUDY UP.

YOU'VE DONE YOUR ANALYSIS AND NOW IT IS TIME TO WRITE UP.!

YOU ARE GOING TO USE FRAMES, KEEPING IN MIND THE IDEA OF ZOOMING OUT.

BIG IMPLICATIONS

CONCRETE FINDINGS

F = FOCAL SENTENCE. WHAT IS THE STORY OF YOUR DATA IN A NUTSHELL?

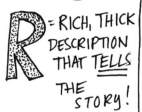

NUTSHELL

"Zorro, a masked hero, defends the people from despotic tyrants."

O

R = RICH, THICK DESCRIPTION THAT <u>TELLS</u> THE STORY!

A hot wind swept across the pueblo. The sun beat down mercilessly on the cracked earth as a few adventurous chickens crept out of the shade to investigate some insects. Dona Flora Acuna had been hanging out some wash to dry and whiten in the bright sunshine, but she hurriedly began to take it down as the red, dusty wind threatened. It was then that she heard the panting of horses and jingling of stirrups in the distance and the hairs on the back of her neck began to stand up. A working woman, Flora had labored all her life, in times of plenty as well as these leaner days, to hold onto her meager holdings here on the outskirts of the pueblo, and she was cautious of bandits. But the tall, capped silhouettes she saw in the hazy distance were more than bandits, they were El Capitan and his gang of so-called "noblemen." Her breath stuck in her throat and her strong, tanned fists tightened on the basket of washing, now tinged with red dust. "Quickly, into the barn!" she shouted to her daughter. The women fled, but not before the riders arrived. "Dona Flora," said the silky smooth voice of El Capitan, "were you running from me?" El Capitan raised his gloved fist when a voice rang out from the cliffs above. "Unhand her!" Flora looked up, hopeful, to see the familiar shape of El Zorro, the fox!

NOTE THE DIFFERENT LANGUAGE.

THE DESCRIPTION LURES IN & FAMILIARIZES THE READER.

THE ANALYSIS INVITES A DEEPER LOOK!

A = ANALYSIS.

Zorro's frequent use of disguise and surprise introduces him as an unpredictable hero, just as El Capitan is an unpredictable villain. The theme of the "unpredictable" nature of life in the pueblo, was often unable to plan. "I just never know when El Capitan is going to show up, steal the grains we set aside for the poor, and slash one of the holy brothers. If I could only plan for these events we would be in much better shape." Similarly, because Zorro was similarly unpredictable force, showing up without warning, and sometimes not at all, participants felt insecure. "I kept thinking, is he going to appear?" asked Dona Susana, "If he is, get on with it already." All participants suggested that a more predictable cycle of violence and salvation would be desirable.

One participant, Friar Tomas, said that because of the unpredictable one at this field site.

SEE HOW THE DATA APPEAR?

WE ZOOM OUT!

M = MEANING →

The idea of the surprise hero being unwelcome is an interesting one. Other studies (Alcalde, 2005; de la Vega, 2010) have explored the extent to which participants who were "saved" have felt nonetheless somewhat angry, or disillusioned, rather than enraptured with or grateful to their particular masked hero. Lolita (1997) and Montero (2001) suggested that this could be interpreted as an aspect of Bahktin's (1929) "carnivalesque" and that by assuming a negative, or even unwelcome, role for the would-be savior, participants are themselves engaged in reframing and deepening understanding of their particular roles in the pueblo "drama." Fairbanks' (2011) study confirmed a similar trend where the stagecoach robbery victims angry attacked the Texas Rangers who came to the rescue.

BUT—
REMEMBER THIS: AS WOLCOTT WROTE OF HIS OWN WRITEUP FORMULA— "THE IDEA PROVIDED A FRAMEWORK... AND I PROPOSE IT AS A WAY TO BOTH EXAMINE STUDIES CONDUCTED BY OTHERS AND TO GUIDE THE TRANSFORMATION OF DATA... AND EVEN NOW I PROPOSE THE IDEA AS A GUIDE, NOT A MAGIC FORMULA" (1994, p. 59)

TO REITERATE...

WRITING THE FOCAL SENTENCE IS YOUR *Fr* INTRO, YOUR HOOK.

THE (R) IS VERY IMPORTANT. MAKE <u>THIS</u> A READ YOUR AUDIENCE JUST CAN'T PUT DOWN!

PRESENTING YOUR ANALYSIS CAN BE AIDED BY USING YOUR THEORY MODEL AS AN ORGANIZER.

EXPAND BY DISCUSSING IMPLICATIONS AND BIG IDEAS.

The implications for current policies around emerging democracies in the Californias are potentially far-reaching. Policymakers must seek the input of all stakeholders, regardless of their positions in the community and their likelihood to rescue and/or pillage from the pueblo, as Wayne and Fonda (2006) demonstrate. Similarly, anthropologists of Wild West Studies should be prepared for the methodological challenges in working with participants whose cultural practices emphasize the value of predictability.

MEANING = "WHAT DOES MY ANALYSIS MEAN?"

AND THEN TELL US WHAT YOUR NEXT STEPS ARE AND SUMMARIZE.

BUT

HERE WE ARE AGAIN...

YOU MAY NOTICE THAT JOURNALS USE A VARIETY OF ORGANIZATIONAL HEADERS.

JOURNAL OF FRENZIED STUDIES

THEY HAVE THEIR OWN CONVENTIONS FOR ACADEMIC ARTICLES. LET'S LOOK AT A FEW.

INTERNATIONAL JOURNAL OF PHLEGMATIC INQUIRY

I. FINDINGS (F, R, A)
II. DISCUSSION (A, M)
III. IMPLICATIONS (E)
IV. CONCLUSION (S)

I. RESULTS (F, R, A)
II. INTERPRETATION (A, M)
III. IMPLICATIONS (M, E)
IV. DISCUSSION (E, S)

I. FINDINGS (F, R, A)
II. THOUGHTS (A)
III. MORE THOUGHTS * (M, F)
IV. SUMMARY (S)

YOU CAN SEE HOW THIS MIGHT KIND OF MATCH UP WITH <u>FRAMES</u>, BUT EVERY JOURNAL IS A LITTLE DIFFERENT.

DATA

just remember that you are zooming out as you discuss, often choosing a few key points to discuss.

✳ THIS IS TOTALLY FOR REAL. THIS IS AN ACTUAL JOURNAL.

Homework № Four

Write for 15 minutes EVERY DAY. I mean it.

get writing

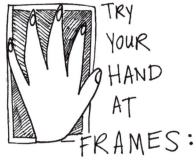

TRY YOUR HAND AT FRAMES:

1. FIRST, LOOK AT YOUR DATA ANALYSIS. WHAT IS THE BASIC STORY OF YOUR DATA? TRY TO GET THAT INTO ONE FOCAL SENTENCE.

2. CHANNEL YOUR INNER NOVELIST. WRITE A RICH, THICK DESCRIPTION OF YOUR STUDY CONTEXT AND THE STORY OF THE DATA.

3. TAKE A STAB AT THE MEANING-MAKING OR ANALYSIS FRAMES. PAY ATTENTION TO HOW THIS FEELS.

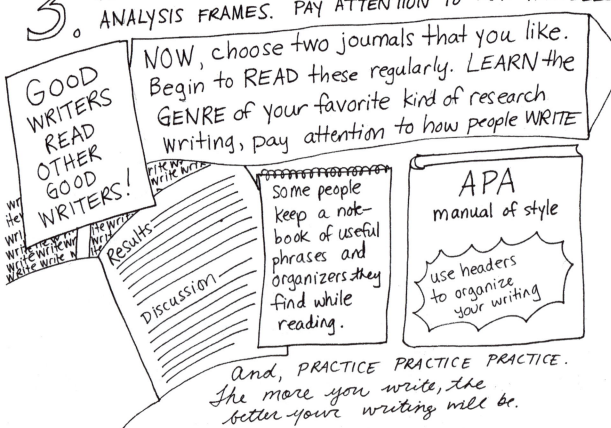

NOW, choose two journals that you like. Begin to READ these regularly. LEARN the GENRE of your favorite kind of research writing, pay attention to how people WRITE

GOOD WRITERS READ OTHER GOOD WRITERS!

Results

Discussion

Some people keep a notebook of useful phrases and organizers they find while reading.

APA manual of style

use headers to organize your writing

and, PRACTICE PRACTICE PRACTICE. The more you write, the better your writing will be.

Chapter Five

THE GREAT TRAIN ROBBERY ...or... DOING NARRATIVE ANALYSIS

Sally Campbell Galman, "The Great Train Robbery... or Doing Narrative Analysis," in *The Good, the Bad, and the Data: Shane the Lone Ethnographer's Basic Guide to Qualitative Data Analysis*, pp. 55-60. © 2013 Left Coast Press, Inc. All rights reserved.

AS MUCH FUN AS BUCKETS AND LABELS CAN BE...

THERE ARE OTHER WAYS OF LOOKING AT DATA

... NOT AS A BODY OF INFORMATION TO BE CODED BUT RATHER A STORY TO UNDERSTAND.

NARRATIVE ANALYSIS is part of the narrative methods tradition, where the object of the analysis is the NARRATIVE, or STORY.

IT AFFIRMS THAT PEOPLES' MEANING-MAKING PROCESSES ARE PART OF STORY CONSTRUCTION. THE STORY IS KEY.

AND THERE IS ALSO AN AUDIENCE*

tell me about a time when...

well...

there was one time when I wa we were all at the beach and I ha towels and flip flops and hot dog bu efore the giant squid an I swam a said wow a whale then I

NARRATIVES APPEAR IN MOST QUALITATIVE DATA.

THOUGH SOME KINDS OF RESEARCH CAN ELICIT THEM.

SOME WITH MORE SUCCESS THAN OTHERS...

is how do you to look at the narrative itself? How do you examine a narrative for meaning?

Of course you can always go ahead and code a narrative.

But there are some special ways to analyze a narrative. Narratives can be "WINDOWS ON DISTINCTIVE SOCIAL WORLDS" (Gubrium & Holstein, 2008, p. 244)

＊THIS IS WHAT MAKES IT A NARRATIVE - A STORY DOESN'T NEED AN AUDIENCE BUT A NARRATIVE DOES!

THERE ARE TWO BASIC WAYS TO LOOK AT NARRATIVES— <u>CONTENT</u> & <u>FORM</u>. (Lieblich et al, 1998). Let's start with a narrative we all know...

The Great Train Robbery

Once upon a time in the Wild West, a pair of robbers decides to rob a train. They force a telegraph operator to send a signal block and trick the engineer into stopping the train. After tying up the telegraph operator, the robbers hide near the tracks and sneak onto the train while it stops and hop inside. However, they are spotted and a firefight begins! The robbers are victorious.

Next, they find the treasure box. But where is the key? A search ensues. They cannot find it! Without the key the robbers are forced to blow open the box with explosives. Suddenly, the train becomes uncoupled and the surprised passengers are forced to leave the train, where they are robbed of their valuables. Then, one of the passengers makes a run for it. He is killed by the robbers who then ride off in the locomotive.

Once safely in the mountains, they disembark, retrieve their horses and prepare a getaway. Meanwhile, the telegraph operator has been loosed from his bonds and runs to find help. A posse of lawmen ride furiously in pursuit of the robbers, quickly finding them. In a hail of bullets, the robbers are killed and the lawmen are victorious.

LABOV's (1972) MODEL LOOKS AT <u>FORM</u>. SO, THE STORIES WE ALL TELL FALL INTO **SIX** PARTS:

snip snip

ABSTRACT (what is this about?)

ORIENTATION (who? what? where?)

COMPLICATION (then what happened?)

RESOLUTION (what finally happened?)

EVALUATION (so what? moral of the story?)

CODA (how does it all end?)

Once upon a time in the Wild West, a pair of robbers decides to rob a train. They force a telegraph operator to send a signal block and trick the engineer into stopping the train. After tying up the telegraph operator, the robbers hide near the tracks and sneak onto the train while it stops and hop inside. However, they are spotted and a firefight begins! The robbers are victorious.

Next, they find the treasure box. But where is the key? A search ensues. They cannot find it! Without the key the robbers are forced to blow open the box with explosives. Suddenly, the train becomes uncoupled and the surprised passengers are forced to leave the train, where they are robbed of their valuables. Then, one of the passengers makes a run for it. He is killed by the robbers who then ride off in the locomotive.

Once safely in the mountains, they disembark, retrieve their horses and prepare a getaway. Meanwhile, the telegraph operator has been loosed from his bonds and runs to find help. A posse of lawmen ride furiously in pursuit of the robbers, quickly finding them. In a hail of bullets, the robbers are killed and the lawmen are victorious.

Once upon a time there was a little girl who lived in the forest with her mother and family. Her granny lived in a cottage some distance away. She did not get a chance to visit her granny very often, so when granny became ill she obviously became thrilled at the chance to venture forth.

She put on her wee little red hood and filled her basket with goodies for sick granny. Her mother warned her that it would be a good idea to move quickly through the very dark wood and absolutely not to stop and talk to strangers. However, the little girl was not terribly keen on listening and as a result was lured into chatting with a big bad wolf. The wolf got all kinds of information out of her and then skipped ahead to her granny's house, where he ate the granny and lay in wait for the girl.

When the girl arrived at her granny's house she knew something was very much amiss but was, again, not a very smart little girl so she went in anyway, and was subsequently devoured. A woodsman nearby heard the ruckus, broke into the house and cut open the wolf to save the girl and her granny from digestion. The end.

Lorem ipsum dolor sit amet, consectetur adipiscing elit. Aenean nec lorem sem, vitae viverra ante. Nunc leo ante, facilisis a semper at, fermentum ac mi. Etiam porttitor malesuada nisl, quis hendrerit nunc lobortis sit amet. Lorem ipsum dolor sit amet, consectetur adipiscing elit. Vestibulum tortor dolor, semper eu euismod a, pharetra nec justo. Maecenas id quam ac sapien vestibulum ornare eu ac purus. Vestibulum quis ligula tellus, ac porta nunc. Praesent nec laoreet ipsum. Donec nulla arcu, ultricies at dignissim feugiat, placerat vel neque. Vestibulum ante ipsum primis in faucibus orci luctus et ultrices posuere cubilia Curae; Sed et augue non nulla tristique pellentesque nec et nisi. Pellentesque sollicitudin magna eget metus placerat laoreet. In lacus orci, ultrices sit amet varius vel, scelerisque sit amet leo. Etiam hendrerit, neque nec lobortis pretium, mi neque venenatis dui, a faucibus turpis tortor eget neque. Duis sed neque tortor, vel sagittis justo. Nullam nec condimentum risus. Pellentesque vulputate dui in mauris auctor sodales. Nulla enim lectus, tristique in auctor ut, semper eu lectus. Cras in ante

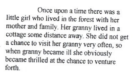

NOW IMAGINE YOU HAVE A LOT OF DIFFERENT NARRATIVES. YOU CAN USE LABOV'S MODEL TO COMPARE, CONTRAST AND ANALYZE THE *FORM*

THESE ARE SOME EXAMPLES OF WHAT LIEBLICH ET AL (1998) CALL "FORM" ELEMENTS. (THINGS ABOUT HOW IT IS WRITTEN)

THESE CONTRAST WITH "CONTENT" ELEMENTS (THINGS ABOUT WHAT IS WRITTEN.)

FURTHER WE CAN LOOK AT FORM AND CONTENT IN HOLISTIC OR PART.

THE WHOLE STORY

ONLY PART OF THE STORY

THINK OF THESE MODES OF ANALYSIS AS THE BIG FOUR.

1. HOLISTIC - CONTENT → compare the narratives as a whole to each other. Ask, what are the narratives each about? How are the stories the same or different?

The Great Train Robbery is about robbers getting their just desserts.

CHOO CHOO

What are the narratives AS A WHOLE about? What happens?

Little Red Riding Hood is about a little girl who becomes dessert.

2. HOLISTIC- FORM is where one looks at the stories as a whole but only as to FORM (think about Labov's parts). Compare the SHAPE of the narratives.

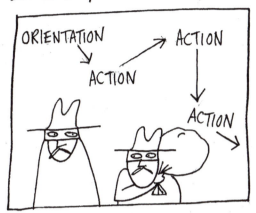

THE NARRATIVES' SHAPES ARE QUITE SIMILAR!

3. PART- CONTENT is where one looks at only PART of the story (rather than the whole thing) with regard to what is IN the story — themes, characters, etc.

villain = masked bandit who robs a train.

THE NARRATIVES EACH USE A VILLAIN, BUT THE VILLAINS ARE THE PROTAGONISTS IN ONE STORY. (QUALITIES ARE DIFFERENT)

Villain = ravenous wolf who eats grannies.

RAHR!

COFFEY & ATKINSON (1996) SUGGEST THAT SOME VERY COMPELLING PART- CONTENT ANALYSES MIGHT EXAMINE THE NARRATIVES' USE OF METAPHOR AND WORDS. THEY ALSO POINT OUT THAT WITH NARRATIVE ANALYSIS, "... FORM AND CONTENT CAN BE STUDIED TOGETHER. A NARRATIVE APPROACH CAN HELP ALERT THE ANALYST TO RESEARCH PROBLEMS AND THEMES THAT CODING AND CONTENT ANALYSIS MAY NOT UNCOVER." (83)

4. PART—FORM: THIS LOOKS AT SMALL <u>PARTS</u> OF THE STORY, BUT NOT PARTS OF WHAT THE STORY IS ABOUT— RATHER, THESE ARE <u>PARTS</u> OF THE <u>FORM</u>. (think Labov)

FOR EXAMPLE—

THE <u>RESOLUTION</u> PART OF EACH STORY IS ABOUT THE DEATH OF THE VILLAIN!

MORBID!

DEAD TRAIN ROBBER

$#

That was a bit abrupt, wasn't it?

Better to get to work!

HOMEWORK Nº.5

Because all this abstract talk about narrative could use some focus!

1. GO THROUGH YOUR DATA AND FIND A N A R R A T I V E. Read it many times.

2. THINK ABOUT FORM. TAKE THE NARRATIVE APART BY USING LABOV'S MODEL.

3. THINK ABOUT <u>CONTENT</u>. WHAT <u>HAPPENS</u> IN THE STORY? WHAT METAPHORS ARE IN PLACE?

4. WRITE UP A MEMO ABOUT HOW THIS KIND OF ANALYSIS CHANGES HOW YOU READ OR EXPERIENCE YOUR DATA.

an important caveat:
"the value of such analytic approaches is in the OPPORTUNITY they afford us to think about the experiences of SOCIAL ACTORS in their own terms. The "DOWN SIDE" of such approaches is that we should ENDEAVOR not to impose our own meanings and imagery." (Coffey & Atkinson 1996 p.106)

Sally Campbell Galman, "The Discourse Kid," in *The Good, the Bad, and the Data: Shane the Lone Ethnographer's Basic Guide to Qualitative Data Analysis*, pp. 61-67. © 2013 Left Coast Press, Inc. All rights reserved.

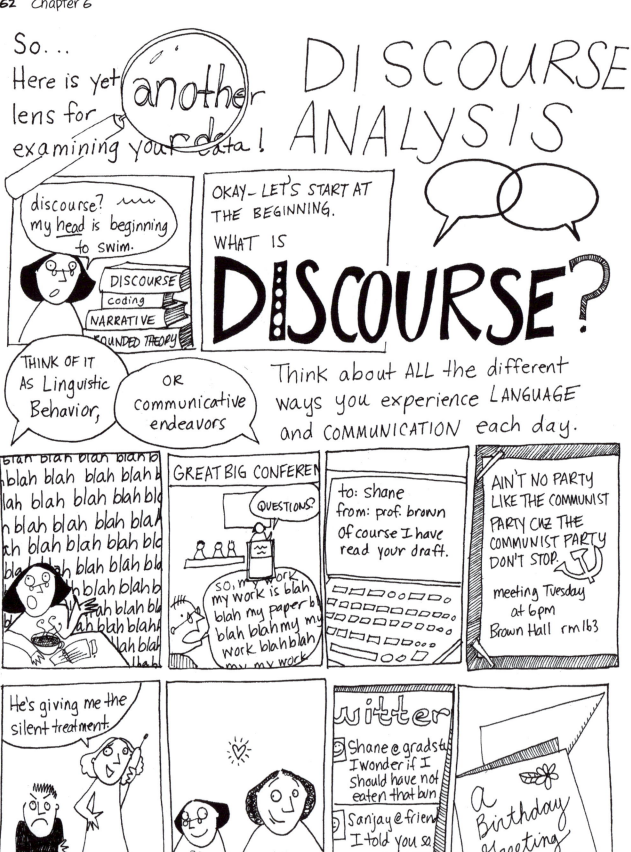

How DO YOU LOOK AT WHAT IS SAID AND HOW IT IS SAID?

How to represent this ↗

rather than this? ↓

stick 'em up.
You stick 'em up.
no you
no you
no you
ah.

We know that when words are spoken there is more to them than this. They are NOT just FLAT WORDS.

How DO YOU SHOW THIS SO YOU CAN ANALYZE IT?

DISCOURSE ANALYSTS USE MANY TOOLS TO REPRESENT DISCOURSE.

One common tool is: Jeffersonian Notation.

(Jefferson, 1984)

— — — — — cut here to add this ABRIDGED VERSION to your cookbook - - - ✂ - - -

hhh	H's	audible exhalation.
,	comma	temporary rise & fall in intonation
[text]	brackets	overlapping speech
=	equal sign	break/continuance of utterance
(# of seconds)	timed pause	pause in speech
(.)	micropause	short pause in speech
. ↓	period or arrow	falling pitch in intonation
? ↑	question or arrow	rising pitch or intonation
—	hyphen	sudden halt or interruption
>text<	greater/less than	rapid speech
<text>	less/greater than	slow speech
°	degree	whisper
ALL CAPS	capitals	shouted speech
(text)	parentheses	speech unclear
((text))	double paren.	non-verbal activity

REMEMBER, THIS IS JUST A SHORT LIST. READ JEFFERSON & OTHERS FOR MORE.

SO, I TRANSCRIBE NOT JUST WHAT IS BEING SAID BUT ALSO HOW IT IS BEING SAID.

HEY- STICK 'EM UP↑ (#3) ALL the way up (hhh) (.) UP↑

WHAT WOULD IT TELL YOU IF HE'D WHISPERED?

This is taking a very, very long time, though. How many times do I have to listen to the VERY SAME THING?

YES. IT TAKES A VERY LONG TIME.

(hhh) = (#2) if I KNEW↓ so he (.) went to the store (.) (hhh)

BUT THE RESULTS CAN BE VERY RICH.

Let's review the steps:
1. Audio/Videotape/Record
2. Transcribe. Be accurate.
3. Listen, listen, listen.
4. Listen with others.
5. Make transcripts even MORE accurate.
6. Read and focus on meaning

But let's see how it works for one scholar.

SMARTY PANTS EXPERT TIP   No 6

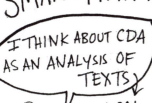

I THINK ABOUT CDA AS AN ANALYSIS OF TEXTS

- ORAL
- WRITTEN
- MULTI MEDIA!

KATRINA DOES CDA - ONE KIND OF DA, WITH ITS OWN ASSUMPTIONS AND PURPOSES. REMEMBER: DA IS NOT ALWAYS CRITICAL OR GEARED TOWARD UNDERSTANDING.

Meet Dr. Katrina Daly Thompson.

Linguist, Africanist, CDA-er

SHE LOOKS AT TEXTS WITH AN EYE TOWARD HOW LANGUAGE & POWER INTERSECT...

... LOOKING AT BOTH BIG ISSUES OF POWER & SOCIETY... AND MICRO ISSUES OF LANGUAGE USE.

I DO MOST OF MY WORK WITH SWAHILI TEXTS TO SEE HOW SWAHILI USERS CONSTRUCT ETHNICITY, GENDER, SEXUALITY & RELIGION.

SO...
Step No ONE:
"WHAT POWER ISSUES AM I INTERESTED IN?"

Step **TWO:**

"What TEXTS MIGHT HELP ME <u>see</u> THAT KIND of POWER?"

OR SOMETIMES I COME ACROSS A TEXT THAT SHOWS AN INTERESTING RELATIONSHIP TO POWER AND SO I JUST COLLECT MORE TEXTS FROM THAT GENRE.

FOR EXAMPLE, DURING MY OWN ISLAMIC WEDDING, I NOTICED HOW SWAHILI WOMEN CONSTRUCT FEMININITY.

... THROUGH LECTURING THE BRIDE AND PRESENTING THEMSELVES AS AUTHORITATIVE BY USING RELIGIOUS DISCOURSE.

I WENT ON FROM THERE TO FURTHER EXPLORE THIS PRACTICE TO BETTER UNDERSTAND THE ISSUES IN PLAY.

I INTERVIEW...

I TRANSCRIBE THE INTERVIEWS... FIRST WITH A ROUGH TRANSCRIPTION THAT ALLOWS ME TO SEE RECURRING THEMES OR INTERESTING USES OF LANGUAGE

WHEN I FIND A SEGMENT THAT NEEDS CLOSER SCRUTINY, I DO A MORE DETAILED TRANSCRIPTION THAT INCLUDES TIMED PAUSES, OVERLAPPING SPEECH, VOWEL-LENGTHENING, PITCH, VOLUME, SILENCES AND SO ON.

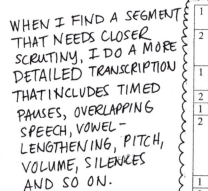

1	The days of the weddi:ng itself, what were they like?
2	@@ On the wedding days, my elders celebrated, @@ then dances were put on, then I was marrie- then I was taken @@@.
1	But isn't it the case that at fi::rst you were taken to someone like Asha will be taken?
2	Yeah, I was taken to be instructed.
1	Where were you taken?
2	I was take:n— Because I was married in Dar es Salaam. So I was picked up and and taken to Temeke to our relatives. And then I was taught all about matters related to the wedding.
1	Mhm.
2	<VOX>It will be like this, it will be like this</VOX> @@.
1	[...]

I BECAME INTERESTED IN CDA BECAUSE IT LETS ME LOOK AT AFRICAN LANGUAGES WITH LARGER SOCIAL ISSUES.

BECAUSE I BELIEVE THAT LANGUAGE BOTH REFLECTS AND IS CONSTRAINED BY POWER RELATIONS.

AND I AM INTERESTED IN DISCOURSE BECAUSE I BELIEVE IN THE IMPORTANCE OF STUDYING LANGUAGE IN CONTEXT.

Zimbabwe's Cinematic Arts: Language, Power, Identity. by Katrina Daly Thompson

time to practice

HOMEWORK №6
○ TRY ○ YOUR ○ HAND ○ AT ○ SOME ○ DA ~

1. GO BACK TO YOUR AUDIO OR VIDEO RECORDINGS.

but I already practiced!

2. PICK A SMALL PIECE. LISTEN TO IT AGAIN. IN FACT, LISTEN SEVERAL TIMES. THINK VERY HARD.

but I already transcribed!

3. AGAIN, FOCUSING ON A VERY SMALL PIECE OF THE RECORDING, TRY YOUR HAND AT JEFFERSONIAN NOTATION,

:: – [text] = (# 2) . ↓? ↑ – > text< <text> ○ (hhh)#

hmm... this is actually kinda' cool...

Pay attention to how this process FEELS. How is it changing how you LISTEN?

What do you notice about yourself as a listener? As a thinker?

new ideas!

4. WHEN YOU HAVE FINISHED, LISTEN A FEW MORE TIMES, AND FINE-TUNE THIS MINI-TRANSCRIPT.

I've learned more about my data!

5. NOW SIT BACK AND THINK. WHAT DO YOU SEE? WHAT KINDS OF WORDS, SOUNDS, PATTERNS AND IDEAS JUMP OUT AT YOU?

remember: this is just a SMALL taste of DA. READ ON!

ANALYZING AND UNDERSTANDING "OTHER KINDS" OF DATA.

Sally Campbell Galman, "Analyzing and Understanding "Other Kinds" of Data," in *The Good, the Bad, and the Data: Shane the Lone Ethnographer's Basic Guide to Qualitative Data Analysis*, pp. 68-78. © 2013 Left Coast Press, Inc. All rights reserved.

* OF COURSE, THESE ARE ALL KINDS OF TEXTS, BUT WE MEAN WORD-INVOLVED.

SO HOW DO WE ANALYZE SOMETHING THAT ISN'T A TEXT?

Sometimes we can transcribe a video into a text.

and we can code the WORDS.

We must also look at other materials as sources of information.

VIDEO DATA

USING VIDEO HAS SOME REAL ADVANTAGES!

NO MATTER HOW RICH YOUR OBSERVATIONAL FIELD NOTES, VIDEO CAN GIVE US MORE NUANCED NON-VERBAL INFO!

LOOK — SIGH — SHRUG — FIDGET — SHUFFLE

 BUT EVEN THE SMALLEST CAMERA CAN BE OBTRUSIVE

AND ALL THAT VIDEO YOU TOOK MUST BE TRANSCRIBED.

SOME TECHNOLOGIES ALLOW ONE TO SEE THE VIDEO AND DO TRANSCRIPTION AT THE SAME TIME, AS IN A SPLIT-SCREEN

HEY! WHAT IS THAT!?

EITHER WAY YOU'LL BE WATCHING THE VIDEO A LOT.

ZZZZZ*

*NOT THAT YOUR WORK ISN'T THRILLING.

ONE STRATEGY TO HELP WITH VIDEO TRANSCRIPTION IS TO BRACKET "ZONES" TO WATCH, OR LOOK AT VERY SPECIFIC KINDS OF INTERACTIONS TO HELP NARROW YOUR FOCUS AND MAKE THINGS MANAGEABLE.

cut out for your COOKBOOK.

ONE CAN OPT FOR

HIGHER AND

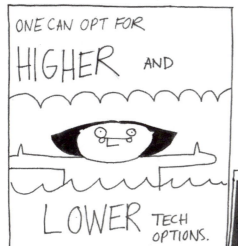

LOWER TECH OPTIONS.

IF THE PIECE CAN BE COPIED, SHRUNK & SCANNED AS A PDF OR PHOTOGRAPH— SOME COMPUTER PROGRAMS WILL LET YOU SELECT AND MAKE NOTES.

FOR LOWER-TECH, GET A TRANSPARENT FILM OVERLAY AND WRITE OVER THE IMAGE.

THEN YOU CODE AS YOU MIGHT NORMALLY DO.

THIS <u>DOES</u> REQUIRE A BIT OF A SHIFT IN YOUR FOCUS— WE SPEND A LOT OF TIME WITH A FOCUS ON WORDS. TEACHING ONESELF TO <u>SEE</u> <u>IMAGES</u> WILL TAKE PRACTICE. IT MIGHT COME EASIER TO SOME AND BE HARDER FOR OTHERS!

YOU MIGHT WANT TO FRAME YOUR CODES AND CONCEPTS FOR <u>IMAGES</u> FROM THE START.

LET'S *Practice* A BIT!

IMAGINE A GROUP OF CHILDREN VISIT THE RANCH FOR A SCHOOL TRIP.

AFTER THEIR VISIT THEY ALL DRAW PICTURES OF WHAT THEY SAW.

HOW WILL YOU USE THE IMAGES TO HELP YOU UNDERSTAND THEIR EXPERIENCE?

SO — unwieldy data can tell us a GREAT DEAL about MEANING in the study CONTEXT BUT... *THERE IS ALWAYS A BUT*

Visual data & artifacts are TRICKY. Your interpretations need CHECKING.

sensitivity MUST be paid to HOW different image and object-producers INSCRIBE MEANING, and how viewers INTERPRET (Pink, 2001)

AND WE NEVER ANALYZE DATA IN A VACUUM!

VAC-O-VAC

NOW IT IS TIME FOR

SMARTY PANTS TIP

☆ Nº SEVEN ☆

MEET DR. FLORENCE SULLIVAN! DR. SULLIVAN ASKS QUESTIONS ABOUT STUDENT COLLABORATIVE LEARNING AND THE ROLE OF TECHNOLOGY IN LEARNING ENVIRONMENTS She uses VIDEO DATA!

DR. SULLIVAN VIDEOTAPES STUDENTS IN COLLABORATIVE INTERACTIONS WITH EACH OTHER...

...THE TEACHER..

AND

THE TECHNOLOGY!

... AND SHE CREATES WRITTEN TRANSCRIPTS OF STUDENT DIALOGUE AND DESCRIPTIONS OF STUDENT ACTIONS IN THE LEARNING ENVIRONMENT.

"VIDEOTAPED INTERACTIONS PROVIDE ME THE OPPORTUNITY TO CREATE A MOMENT-BY-MOMENT ANALYSIS OF MANY OF THE FACTORS THAT WERE PRESENT WHEN THE LEARNING ACTIVITY WAS TAKING PLACE.

VIDEO ALLOWS ME TO DO A CLOSE ANALYSIS BY REWINDING AND REWATCHING THE INTERACTION!"

IT IS IMPORTANT TO NOTE THAT EVEN A VIDEO RECORD IS PARTIAL — THE CAMERA ONLY CAPTURES ONE VIEW. IT ISN'T DEFINITIVE!

BUT IN A VIDEO I CAN WATCH AS LEARNING DEVELOPS!

AND, I CAN VERIFY MY INTERPRETATION WITH OTHERS WHO CAN ALSO VIEW THE TAPE.

TO ANALYZE VIDEO DATA, I CREATE A DETAILED TRANSCRIPT WITH

⤳ SPOKEN DIALOGUE

⤳ DESCRIPTIONS OF ACTION

⤳ TIME STAMPS.

I HAVE TO WATCH THE VIDEO MANY TIMES TO CONSTRUCT SUCH A TRANSCRIPT.

IT IS TIME-CONSUMING AND TEDIOUS, BUT THE ANALYSIS BENEFITS FROM A <u>RICH</u> TRANSCRIPT.

I LIKE TO USE EXCEL BECAUSE THE MATRIX STRUCTURE LETS ME LOOK AT MORE THAN ONE FACTOR AT ONCE.

AFTER TRANSCRIBING, I APPLY A THEORETICALLY-BASED CODING SCHEME, TO <u>BOTH</u> WORDS AND ACTIONS.

DON'T FORGET:

▭ USE WIRELESS MICROPHONES TO ASSURE SOUND QUALITY.

▭ BACK UP YOUR SOURCE DATA IN MULTIPLE PLACES.

▭ TEST OUT YOUR EQUIPMENT TO BE SURE IT'S ALL WORKING!

Excel File Edit View Insert Format Tools Data Window Help

A2 — fx Group Activity

PositioningAnalysis.xlsx

Verdana — 10 — B I U

	A	B	C	D	E	F	G
1	Positioning Analysis - Day One	00:00:00-00:05:00	00:05:00-00:10:00	00:10:00-00:15:00	00:15:00-00:20:00	00:20:00-00:25:00	00:25:00-00:30:00
2	Group Activity	Class setting - Introduce the researchers	Introduce activity	Show robot - make groups	People move into groups, Mr. Smith does some moving around of groups	Students get kits and begin first activity (find and draw pieces).	Students work on first activity.
3	Control of Laptop						
4	Control of Robotic Device					20:00 - Javier retrieves the kit when Mr. Smith tells students to get the kits.	
5	Control of Pieces						Shared throughout activity segment.
6	Control of Worksheet/Ruler						
	Positioning Statements			11:00 - Mr. Smith - introduces his computer as Schneider and refers to it as "he." Mr. Smith also discusses the fact that some of the students may recognize this robot because it is the same one they are using in Robotics for Boys - so right off the bat, the boys are positioned as potentially knowing more AND the inanimate object is referred to as male.		23:00 - Ilana looks into the orange pieces bin and mentions that the pieces are also used in Robotics for Girls and then Javier says "We are building this in Robotics for boys, too."	27:50 - Sara states the activity is "easy." 29:00 Sara working with a piece says "I don't know."

Sheet1

Normal View   Ready   SCRL CAPS NUM

HOMEWORK NUMBER SEVEN 7

LOOK THROUGH YOUR DATA. DO YOU HAVE PHOTOS, VIDEO, ETC.?

MAKE A LIST OF ALL SUCH DATA.

1. _____
2. _____
3. _____
4. _____

FILL OUT PLACE-HOLDER FORMS.

NOW — EITHER SCAN, PHOTOGRAPH, WATCH OR USE TRANSPARENCIES TO CODE.

THINK ABOUT:

→ WHAT KINDS OF IMAGES ARE PRESENT? _MISSING?_

→ WHAT KINDS OF IMAGES/OBJECTS/OTHER CUES CORRESPOND TO YOUR CONCEPTUAL BUCKETS AND/OR CODEBOOK.

WRITE:

→ MEMOS ABOUT WHAT YOU SEE AND WHAT YOU THINK.

→ A THOROUGH DESCRIPTION OF THE DATA. THIS COULD BE AN EXPANSION ON WHAT IS ON THE PLACEHOLDER FORM.

BUT I DON'T HAVE ANY DATA LIKE THIS! WHAT DO I DO?

PRACTICE PAYING ATTENTION TO IMAGES IN YOUR ENVIRONMENT. THINK ABOUT WHAT YOU SEE.

PAY ATTENTION TO OBJECTS AND ARTIFACTS AND HOW THEY ARE USED... AND WHAT THAT MIGHT MEAN!

Sally Campbell Galman, "Calamity Shane," in *The Good, the Bad, and the Data: Shane the Lone Ethnographer's Basic Guide to Qualitative Data Analysis*, pp. 79-86. © 2013 Left Coast Press, Inc. All rights reserved.

K is for KICKING YOURSELF because you did not tidy up properly and finished analysis only to find a pile of files you forgot. (do it again)

DARN.

L is for LAZY. You didn't transcribe everything. You will regret this. Your analysis will suffer. Go back and RecTIEy...

I'LL JUST LISTEN...

M IS FOR METHODOLOGY MEANINGLESSNESS.

DON'T JUST "PICK" — — UNDERSTAND.

I'll do GROUNDED THEORY!

what's that?

N IS FOR NOTHING.

Yes, it is a problem if you find nothing

O IS FOR OH NO! I didn't OBSERVE!

All you have are notes that are your interpretation of events rather than actual observations.

Jim was irritating me today. He is really irritated. He seems

P Is for PROCRASTINATION.

what was I doing here?

don't let too much time pass before you analyze.

Q is for QUIXOTIC QUESTION

oopsie. You didn't answer your actual research question.

Retweak or Redo your analysis...

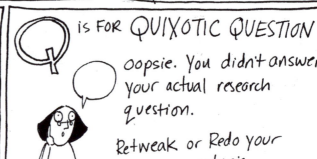

R IS FOR REPETITIVE RESULT.

NOOO! MY FINDINGS HAVE ALREADY BEEN FOUND! (DO A BETTER LIT REVIEW!)

(But don't freak out— maybe a new WRINKLE on the same subject is afoot...)

S is for SENTIMENT.

is your analysis colored by sentiment?

but my participants are so NOBLE!

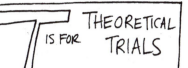 **T IS FOR THEORETICAL TRIALS**

DID YOU OPERATIONALIZE YOUR THEORY SO YOU CAN REALLY USE IT?

DO YOU KNOW WHAT YOUR THEORY LOOKS LIKE?

 **U gh! USELESS CODES! UNINTELLIGIBLE!**

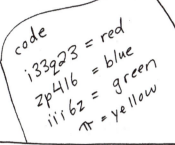

code
i33q23 = red
zp416 = blue
iii6z = green
π = yellow

V ERY VERY BORED.

DATA COLLECTION IS SHODDY BECAUSE YOU GOT BORED.

ANALYSIS IS TORTURE BECAUSE YOU GOT BORED.

W IS FOR WANDERING WOMB SYNDROME

Are your assumptions and theories antiquated or bizarre?

I have proven spontaneous generation and witchcraft!

X IS FOR EXTRA STUFF!

You completed your analysis and you have all this extra data that does not seem to fit. Maybe it's time to revisit your questions and design.

extra data

Y IS FOR YECCCH!

I don't like my findings, participants, setting, etc. etc. Read The Mountain People (Turnbull, 1972) and be chastened.

Z IS FOR ZEALOTRY.

DID you make room for discovery or did you only confirm your own rigid ideas?

these are the ONLY possible findings. I AM SURE.

MISTAKES YOU MAKE IN ANALYSIS = FIX BY REDOING!
MISTAKES IN DESIGN/COLLECTION = BACK TO THE FIELD!

Remember, it is all data, and you are always learning!  sigh

SHARPEN YOUR PENCILS & YOUR BRAIN BECAUSE IT IS...

HOMEWORK No. 8

I MEAN, REALLY. WHY WAIT FOR A CATASTROPHIC ERROR TO HARSH YOUR BUZZ?

THIS IS REALLY A CHECKLIST. BE PROACTIVE!

- ☐ Go back and make sure you were thorough in your tidying up. Make sure all the data is transcribed, and doublecheck the inventory.

- ☐ Invest in subjectivity management strategies. Memo, journal, talk to critical friends, read other perspectives and record your thoughts so you aren't surprised by your own assumptions.

- ☐ Make a data analysis matrix. (see LeCompte & Schensul, 1999). This will help assure that your theories are well-operationalized and that your coding is consistent.

- ☐ Do some deep reading on the data analysis strategies you are using. Make sure you really understand both what you are doing and why.

- ☐ Make a NOTE of "exciting" findings and dedicate special time to a search for disconfirming or complicating data.

- ☐ Have a colleague "test drive" your codebook. Then you'll weed out bad codes or weird, antiquated concepts.

- ☐ Be honest with yourself. If you have sketchy data that might not be as useable as it should be, you may need to go back to the field.

Sally Campbell Galman, "Time to Hit the Old Dusty Audit Trail," in *The Good, the Bad, and the Data: Shane the Lone Ethnographer's Basic Guide to Qualitative Data Analysis*, pp. 87-96. © 2013 Left Coast Press, Inc. All rights reserved.

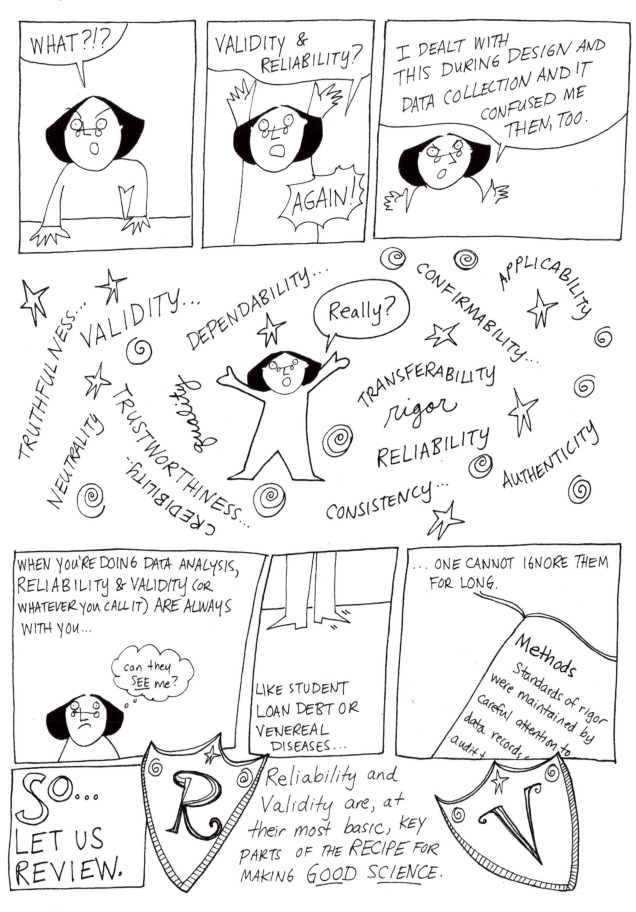

THEY DO ULTIMATELY COME OUT OF THE POSITIVIST CANON...

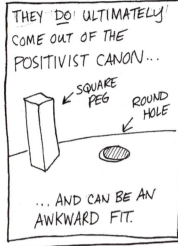

← SQUARE PEG

ROUND HOLE →

...AND CAN BE AN AWKWARD FIT.

BUT WE FOLLOW THEM AS STANDARDS OF RIGOR, IN SPIRIT AND DIRECTION.

THIS WAY →

RELIABILITY

OLD PAINT HERE IS SO UNRELIABLE. HIS PERFORMANCE IS INCONSISTENT, AND I AM NEVER SURE IF HE WILL HOLD UP!

OLD PAINT IS AN UNRELIABLE CONVEYANCE BECAUSE HE IS NOT CONSISTENT OVER TIME AND HIS PERFORMANCE MAY BE INCOMPLETE.

STUDY RESULTS THAT ARE RELIABLE ARE CONSISTENT OVER TIME AND ARE REASONABLY COMPLETE REPRESENTATIONS OF THE POPULATION AT HAND.

THEY SHOULD ALSO BE GENERALLY REPLICABLE— MEANING SIMILAR RESULTS SHOULD APPEAR IN SIMILAR SETTINGS IF REPEATED.

BUT WAIT! IN NATURALISTIC STUDIES WE DON'T VALUE BEING ABLE TO REPRODUCE RESULTS! HA! SO THERE!

FINDINGS NEED NOT BE GENERALIZABLE IN ORDER TO BE RELIABLE...

THOUGH RESULTS SHOULD SUPPORT & INFORM OTHER WORK.

AND CONSISTENCY MEANS THAT ANALYSIS AND COLLECTION CAN BE SHOWN TO HAVE BEEN CAREFULLY AND MINDFULLY DONE.

LIKE A CAKE BATTER— IT MUST BE CONSISTENT. NO LUMPS.

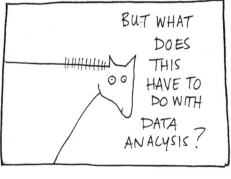

BUT WHAT DOES THIS HAVE TO DO WITH DATA ANALYSIS?

THREATS TO RELIABILITY:

1. INATTENTION TO DETAIL

I THINK WE CAN STOP HERE— WE HAVE KIND OF A BIG ENOUGH SET OF INTERVIEWS...

2. POOR RECORDING OF THE PROCESS.

UM... WHEN DID I DO THAT? DID I DO THAT?

3. FUZZY PROCEDURES

I'M NOT SURE IF I ASKED ALL THE SAME QUESTIONS IN ALL 12 INTERVIEWS...

REMEMBER, WE ARE NOT REPLICATING RESULTS. IT CAN'T BE DONE IN NATURALISTIC WORK.

4. FAILURE TO BE CLEAR.

WELL— THAT SEEMS LIKE THE SAME THING AS THE OTHER CONCEPT... SURE, THROW IT IN...

NOW... VALIDITY!

RESEARCH QUESTION= "HOW MANY HAIRS ON OLD PAINT'S HEAD?"

FINDING= "I'VE DISCOVERED COLD FUSION!"

VALIDITY PROBLEM.

VALIDITY DETERMINES WHETHER THE RESEARCH REALLY MEASURES WHAT IT IS CLAIMING TO MEASURE. IT CANNOT BE VALID — WHICH IS TO SAY TRUTHFUL — IF THAT IS CONFUSED.

ASK YOURSELF...

DID I REALLY EXAMINE WHAT I THINK I EXAMINED?

PEOPLE USUALLY AREN'T KIDDING THEMSELVES— BUT SOMETIMES QUESTIONS AND CONCEPTS GET CONFUSED.

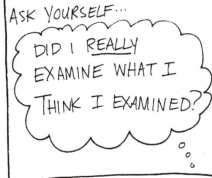

CLUMSY CONCEPTS

FOR EXAMPLE, IF YOU ONLY ASK QUESTIONS ABOUT HORSES BUT THEN CLAIM TO SPEAK ABOUT CHICKENS, YOU HAVE PROBLEMS.

SO... WHAT DOES THIS MEAN FOR YOU AS YOU DO DATA ANALYSIS? THERE IS A LOT TO ATTEND TO, BUT LET'S FOCUS ON TWO IMPORTANT SAFEGUARDS:

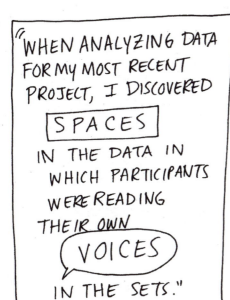

"WHEN ANALYZING DATA FOR MY MOST RECENT PROJECT, I DISCOVERED SPACES IN THE DATA IN WHICH PARTICIPANTS WERE READING THEIR OWN VOICES IN THE SETS."

THIS WAS MORE THAN "MEMBER CHECKS," OR "VALIDITY MEASURES"

PARTICIPANTS WERE FORMING A LAYER IN THE GENERATION AND DEVELOPMENT OF DATA.

THEY WERE REVISITING THEMSELVES IN THE DATA...

LOOKING FOR THEIR VOICES AND OTHERS.'

THEY WERE RECORDING THEMSELVES DOING THIS WORK.

They also wrote about their journals and their processes of revisiting the data to find something they remembered or needed to clarify.

"THIS ADDED DIMENSION TO THE DATA... THE PARTICIPANTS WERE DOING THIS WORK IN ORDER TO SPEAK TO A DESIRE FOR THE RECOGNITION OF VOICE(S), TO FORM NEW LITERACY EVENTS... THEY ROSE UP IN THE DATA THROUGH TALK AND WRITING."

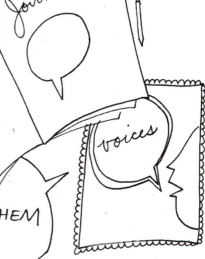

"I HONOR MY PARTICIPANTS IN THE PROCESS OF ANALYSIS BY INVITING THEM INTO THE ANALYTIC SPACE I CREATE."

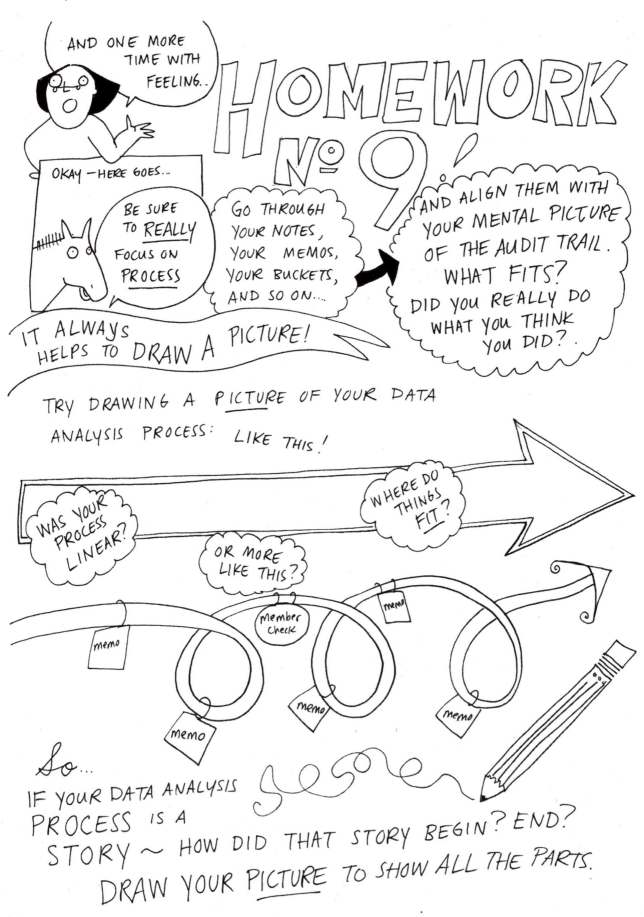

Sally Campbell Galman, "Our Hero Takes Her Final Bow," in *The Good, the Bad, and the Data: Shane the Lone Ethnographer's Basic Guide to Qualitative Data Analysis*, pp. 97-99. © 2013 Left Coast Press, Inc. All rights reserved.

Bruner, J. S. (1990). *Acts of meaning.* Cambridge, MA: Harvard University Press.

Cahnmann-Taylor, M., Wooten, J., Souto-Manning, M., & Dice, J. (2009). The art & science of educational inquiry: Analysis of performance-based focus groups with novice bilingual teachers. *Teachers College Record, 111*(11), 2535-2559.

Clandinin, D. J., & Connelly, F. M. (2000). *Narrative inquiry: Experience and story in qualitative research.* San Francisco: Jossey-Bass Publishers.

Campbell, T. (1996). Technology, multimedia, and qualitative research in education. *Journal of Research on Computing in Education, 30*(9), 122-133.

Coffey, A., & Atkinson, P. (1996). *Making sense of qualitative data: Complementary research strategies.* Thousand Oaks: SAGE.

Connelly, F. M. and Clandinin, D. J. (1990). Stories of experience and narrative inquiry. *Educational Researcher, 19*(5), 2–14.

Creswell, J. W. & Miller, D. L. (2000). Determining validity in qualitative inquiry. *Theory into Practice, 39*(3), 124-131.

Daly Thompson, K. (2012). *Zimbabwe's cinematic arts: Language, power, identity.* Bloomington: Indiana University Press.

Daly Thompson, K. (2011). How to be a good Muslim wife: Women's performance of Islamic authority during Swahili weddings. *Journal of Religion in Africa 41*(4), 427-448.

Daly Thompson, K. (2010). "I Am Maasai": Interpreting ethnic parody in Bongo Flava. *Language in Society, 39*(4), 493–520.

Daly Thompson, K. (2008). Keeping it real: Reality and representation in Maasai Hip-Hop. *Journal of African Cultural Studies 20* (1), 33-44. Special Issue on East Africa.

Fairclough, N. (2003). *Analysing discourse: Textual analysis for social research.* New York: Routledge.

Galman, S. (2007). *Shane the lone ethnographer: A beginner's guide to ethnography.* Lanham, MD: AltaMira Press.

Galman, S. (2009). The truthful messenger: Visual methods and representation in qualitative research in education. *Qualitative Research 9*(197), 197–217.

Geertz, C. (1973). *The interpretation of cultures: Selected essays.* New York: Basic Books.

Glaser, B. G., & Strauss, A. L. (2009). *The discovery of grounded theory: Strategies for qualitative research.* New York: Aldine.

Gubrium, J. F., & Holstein, J. A. (2008). Narrative ethnography. In S. Hesse-Biber & P. Leavy (Eds.), *Handbook of emergent methods* (pp. 241–264). New York: Guilford.

Hirshfield, J. (2007). *After: Poems.* New York: Harper Perennial.

Ives, D. (2011). Spotting foolbirds: Literacies hiding in plain sight in an urban English language arts classroom. *Journal of Literacy Research, 43*(3), 250-274.

Jefferson, G. (1984). Transcript notation. In J. M. Atkinson & J. Heritage (Eds.), *Structures of social action: Studies in conversation analysis* (pp. ix-xvi). Cambridge: Cambridge University Press.

Labov, W. (1972). *Sociolinguistic patterns.* Philadelphia: University of Pennsylvania Press.

LeCompte, M. D., & Schensul, J. J. (1999). *Analyzing and interpreting ethnographic data.* Lanham, MD: AltaMira Press.

Li, Y., & Larsen, D. (2012). Finding hope in the darkness: Stories of two Chinese newcomers enrolled in a Canadian high school. *Canadian and International Education 41*(1), 39-58.

Lieblich, A., Tuval Mashiach, R., and Zilber, T. (1998). *Narrative research: Reading, analysis and interpretation.* Thousand Oaks, CA: SAGE.

Lincoln, Y. S., & Guba, E. G. (1985). *Naturalistic inquiry.* Thousand Oaks, CA: SAGE.

Mallozzi, C. A. (2012). Cultural models of bodily images of women teachers. *Societies* [Special issue: Embodied Action, Embodied Theory: Understanding the Body in Society], 2, 252-269.

Mallozzi, C. A. (2011). Reading women teachers: A theoretical assertion for bodies as texts. *English Teaching: Practice and Critique, 11*(3), 129-141.

Mallozzi, C. A. (2009). Voicing the interview: A researcher's exploration on a platform of empathy. *Qualitative Inquiry, 15,* 1042-1060.

Marshall, B., Staples, J. M., & Gibson, S. (2009). Ghetto fabulous: Reading representations of Black adolescent femininity in contemporary urban street fiction. *Journal of Adolescent and Adult Literacy, 53*(1), 28–36.

Maynard, K. & Cahnmann-Taylor, M. (2010). Anthropology at the edge of words: Where poetry and ethnography meet. *Anthropology & Humanism 35*(1), 2-19.

McClure, G. & Cahnmann-Taylor, M. (2010). Pushing back against push-in; ESOL teacher resistance & the complexities of coteaching. *TESOL journal, 1*(1), 101–129.

Miles, M. B., & Huberman, A. M. (1994). *Qualitative data analysis: An expanded sourcebook.* Thousand Oaks, CA: SAGE.

Nygreen, K. (2013) *These kids: Identity, agency, and social justice at a last chance high school.* Chicago: University of Chicago Press.

Peshkin, A. (1988). Understanding complexity: A gift of qualitative inquiry. *Anthropology & Education Quarterly, 19*(4), 416–424.

Pink, S. (2001). *Doing visual ethnography: Images, media and representation in research.* Thousand Oaks, CA: SAGE.

Pink, S. (2004). *Home truths: Gender, domestic objects and everyday life.* New York: Berg.

Pink, S. (2005). *The future of visual Anthropology: Engaging the Senses.* New York: Routledge.

Rossman, G. B., & Rallis, S. F. (2011). *Learning in the Field: An Introduction to Qualitative Research.* (Third Edition). Thousand Oaks, CA: SAGE.

Schensul, S. L., Schensul, J. J., & LeCompte, M. D. (1999). *Essential ethnographic methods: Observations, interviews, and questionnaires.* Lanham, MD: AltaMira Press.

Staples, J. M. (2012). "Niggaz dyin' don't make no news": Exploring the intellectual work of an African American urban adolescent boy in an after school program. *Educational Action Research, 20*(1), 55–73.

Staples, J. M. (2012). "There are two truths": African American women's critical, creative ruminations on love through new literacies. *Pedagogy, Culture and Society, 20*(3).

Staples, J. M. (2011). The revelation(s) of Asher Levi: An iconographic literacy event as a tool for the exploration of fragmented selves in new literacies studies after 9/11. *Qualitative Studies, 2*(2), 79–97.

Staples, J. M. (2010). "Does my iMovie® suck?": Assessing teacher candidates' digital compositions. *English Journal, 99*(5), 95–99.

Staples, J. M. (2010). Encouraging agitation: Teaching teacher candidates to confront words that wound. *Teacher Education Quarterly, 37*(1), 53–72.

Staples, J. M. (2008). "How do I know what I think 'till I hear what I say?": The role of collaborative discourse in critical media literacy development. *The International Journal of Learning, 15*(7), 107–118.

Strauss, A., & Corbin, J. M. (1990). *Basics of qualitative research: Grounded theory procedures and techniques.* Newbury Park, CA. SAGE.

Sullivan, F.R. (2011). Serious and playful inquiry: Epistemological aspects of collaborative creativity. *Journal of Educational Technology and Society, 14*(1), 55-65.

Sullivan, F.R. (2008). Robotics and science literacy: Thinking skills, science process skills, and systems understanding. *Journal of Research in Science Teaching, 45*(3), 373-394.

Tracy, K., & Mirivel, J.C. (2009). Discourse analysis: The practice and practical value of taping, transcribing, and analyzing talk. In L. R. Frey & K. N. Cissna (Eds.), *Routledge handbook of applied communication research* (pp. 153-177). New York: Routledge.

Turnbull, C. M. (1972). *The Mountain People.* New York: Simon & Schuster.

Wolcott, H. F. (1994). *Transforming qualitative data: Description, analysis, and interpretation.* Thousand Oaks, CA: SAGE.

Wolcott, H. F. (2010). *Ethnography lessons: A primer.* Walnut Creek, CA: Left Coast.

ABOUT THE AUTHOR:

SALLY CAMPBELL GALMAN IS AN
ASSOCIATE PROFESSOR AT THE SCHOOL
OF EDUCATION @ THE UNIVERSITY OF
MASSACHUSETTS AT AMHERST. WHEN
SHE IS NOT BUSY WITH SHANE, SHE TEACHES
QUALITATIVE RESEARCH METHODS
COURSES. SHE LIVES IN AMHERST,
MASSACHUSETTS WITH HER HUSBAND,
MATT, THEIR 3 SMALL CHILDREN AND
THE CATS. www.blogs.umass.edu/sallyg